Aufbauwortschatz Englisch

Vocabulary Exercises

by Christa and Lester Kaplan

Ernst Klett Verlag

Aufbauwortschatz Englisch – Vocabulary Exercises

von Lester Kaplan, M. A. (University of California),
und Christa Kaplan, Wien;
unter Mitwirkung der Verlagsredaktion Weiterbildung Fremdsprachen;
Leiter: Wolfgang H. Kaul, M. A.
Mitarbeit an diesem Werk: Derrick Jenkins, Verlagsredakteur

Acknowledgements

The authors would like to thank students and friends who helped in the preparation of the manuscript, especially Mr Hans Limberger.

ISBN 3-12-519540-3

1. Auflage 1 9 8 7 6 | 1991 90 89 88

Alle Drucke dieser Auflage können im Unterricht nebeneinander benutzt werden, sie sind untereinander unverändert. Die letzte Zahl bezeichnet das Jahr dieses Druckes.

Contents

For the Student

Although the total number of words in the English language is very large — around 500,000 — only a small number of them appear and reappear, again and again, in daily life. For this reason, as Professor Erich Weis has written, a student can easily understand 95% of the words of an average conversation or average written text if he knows the most important 4,500 words of the language. These basic 4,500 words Professor Weis has listed in his book, *Grund- und Aufbauwortschatz Englisch* (Klettbuch 51951), and has divided them into two groups. The first group, the 2,000 words which supply 85% of the words of daily English, is the *Grundwortschatz*. The second group, the 2,500 words which make up another 10% of daily English, is the *Aufbauwortschatz*.

Our exercise book tests the *Aufbauwortschatz* and follows its organization, chapter by chapter. For example, in Chapter I of our book all the words which are tested or written in *italics* (like *this*) are from Chapter I of the *Aufbauwortschatz*.

To make your work easier and more effective, we'd like to offer some suggestions:

Study efficiently. Write your answers on a separate sheet of paper, not in this book. Then look at the answer-keys (which are at the end of each chapter) and put a mark in the book next to each question you answered incorrectly. When you review a chapter a day or two later, do only the questions you marked. Continue to review a chapter until you can answer all questions perfectly.

Work regularly. Studying thirty minutes every day for six days a week will help you more than studying three hours one day a week.

Admit all your mistakes. Many students have the feeling that mistakes are shameful things which should be hidden or forgotten. Actually, mistakes only tell you what has to be practised and reviewed.

Don't give up. If a chapter is difficult for you, close this book, open *Grund- und Aufbauwortschatz Englisch*, study the words of the test-chapter, and then try to do the exercises again.

Set your goals realistically. No student will ever be able to say, "Now I have finished learning English." However, if you work honestly, regularly and seriously with this book, you should be able to say, within a short time, "Now I feel comfortable in English."

For the Teacher

The goal of this book is to give the student a firm command over the most important 4,500 words of the English language, and thereby enable him to understand 95 % of the words of an average conversation or written text. The 4,500-word vocabulary is listed in Professor Erich Weis's book, *Grund- und Aufbauwortschatz Englisch*, which is described in the preceding section, "For the Student".

The words

If a teacher feels that many of the words in this book are new to the students, he may have them study the corresponding chapters of the *Aufbauwortschatz* before doing the exercises; the organization and chapter numbering of this book follow Professor Weis's *Grund- und Aufbauwortschatz Englisch.*

All words in this book written in *italics* are from the corresponding chapter of the *Aufbauwortschatz;* all other words are from the *Grundwortschatz*, the corresponding chapter of the *Aufbauwortschatz*, or are easily recognizable because they

— consist of a *Grundwortschatz* word with an ending such as *-ly* or *-ation* (e. g. *calmly*, *expectation*); or
— consist of a combination of two *Grundwortschatz* words (e. g. *will-power*); or
— are very similar to words used daily in many European languages, including German (e. g. *method*, *rapid*); or
— are international words (e. g. *computer*, *sociology*, *vanilla*, *dynamite*).

A student who finds the non-italicized words too difficult would be well-advised to begin with the companion volume to this book, *Grundwortschatz Englisch — Vocabulary Exercises*, by Lawrence C. Morgan and Roy E. Ogren (Klettbuch 51952).

The questions

Within each chapter, Sections I to VI test the student's passive vocabulary (words he or she can recognize when heard or read but cannot use in speaking or writing). Some of the questions in the first four sections draw attention to points which might mislead native German speakers; for example, the student is made aware that the English word *caution* does not mean "money left as a guarantee for something".

Sections V and VI are designed to increase the student's ability to form associations of

— words with similar meanings, thereby reducing the student's need to repeat the same words again and again when speaking or writing; and
— words which form phrases, such as *by means of;* and
— words which frequently appear in the same context, such as *mirror* and *reflection.*

Sections VII—X test the student's active vocabulary (words which the student can use as well as understand); the questions require the student to supply a particular word within a clear context.

Section IX is of particular importance since it concentrates on one of the most troublesome aspects of our language, the use of prepositions.

Section X, the Review Section, tests words and phrases which appear somewhere in the chapter without having been tested directly, or which appear without a context in Sections V and VI.

The two types of questions, I—VI for the passive vocabulary and VII—X for the active vocabulary, allow the teacher to use the book as a diagnostic tool. If for example a student repeatedly scores "Excellent" and "Good" in Sections I—VI but "Not very good" and "Weak" in VII—IX, his grades indicate that his ability to recognize words is far more advanced than his ability to use them; in practical terms this means the student needs less reading and more writing.

The exercises contained in this book have been tested on several hundred students; however, improvement is always possible and all suggestions and reports of experience will be warmly welcomed.

Vienna, 1976

Chapter I Quantities

Do you know all about *addition*, *subtraction*, *multiplication* and *division?* You do? *That's nothing!* Everyone learns them in school. But do you know how to chat in English? You will — after you finish this book! Why? Because we give you a chance to *eliminate* your mistakes and begin thinking in English!

But the effort must come from you! The *burden* of learning English rests on you, so throw yourself *completely* into the work!

I. What's the opposite?

1. People *consume* what others
   a) produce.
   b) distribute.
   c) use.

2. "You can't tell me that £50,000 is a *trifle!* It's clearly
   a) something important!"
   b) a payment!"
   c) a reward!"

3. Do you believe children need *definite* limits or
   a) infinite ones?
   b) indefinite ones?
   c) inferior ones?

4. Last year she *shortened* her skirts, but this year she
   a) sewed them up.
   b) cut them.
   c) lengthened them.

II. Which word or phrase has almost the same meaning?

1. *Half a dozen* eggs, please.
   a) two
   b) three
   c) six

2. *Six of one, half a dozen of the other.*
   a) Six of these, six of those.
   b) Twelve in total.
   c) It doesn't make any difference.

3. They *enlarged* the town.
   a) increased the size of
   b) stored their things in
   c) surrounded

4. *Total up* the bill, please.
   a) look at
   b) add up
   c) pay

5. The *bulk* of the shipment has been sent.
   a) the first part
   b) the main part
   c) the remaining part

6. Do the difficult exercises *several* times.
   a) three or four times
   b) seven times
   c) again and again

7. He made a *grave* mistake.
   a) slight
   b) very serious
   c) it killed someone

8. What's the machine's *capacity?*
   a) height and length
   b) amount of work it is doing now
   c) maximum amount of work it can do

9. What's the stadium's seating *capacity?*
   a) height and length
   b) number of people in it now
   c) maximum number of seats

10. He knows *innumerable* stories about his old uncle.
    a) countless
    b) a number of
    c) neither numbered nor organized

III. Which choice makes sense?

1. I see the gap
   a) in the wall.
   b) she gave me as a gift.
   c) which is so heavy.

2. You're ten pence off.
   a) How did you lose them?
   b) I'll pick them up from the floor.
   c) I owe you 50 pence, not 60.

3. I think you're completely
   a) fast!
   b) wrong!
   c) hot!

4. The student calculated
   a) his pencils.
   b) the professor's sentence.
   c) the speed of the machine.

5. The priest said we should lessen
   a) our religious feelings.
   b) God for forgiveness.
   c) the world's suffering.

6. Millions of people lost their lives
   a) in the last war.
   b) at the horse-races.
   c) by watching television.

7. I've been listening with only half an ear,
   a) so I have to go to the doctor's.
   b) so say it again, please.
   c) so speak louder.

8. The house is two stories
   a) high.
   b) old.
   c) wide.

If you want to *enlarge* and *widen* your vocabulary, and *deepen* your knowledge in general, you'll have to make the effort! After all, we never promised to *eliminate* your work! But these exercises can *shorten* your road to perfect English.

Don't *subtract* from your work-time! On to the next exercise!

IV. Is it true or false?

	T	F
1. Most cars burn a mixture of petrol and air.	☐	☐
2. The contents of a glass bottle determine its shape.	☐	☐
3. If you have sufficient food, then you have enough.	☐	☐
4. If you have a surplus of food, then you have more than enough.	☐	☐
5. Your breadth is faster when your heart beats faster.	☐	☐
6. A large book contains numerous pages.	☐	☐
7. The stars in the sky are countless.	☐	☐
8. The demand for beef usually diminishes as the price of beef increases.	☐	☐

V. Find the nouns which go together.

1. story
2. burden
3. pile
4. remainder
5. breadth

a) heap, b) rest, c) load, d) length, e) floor

VI. Find the words which go together.

1. a score
2. a couple
3. a dozen
4. half a dozen

a) two, b) six, c) twelve, d) twenty

5. addition
6. subtraction
7. multiplication
8. division

e) $3 \times 2 = 6$, f) $3 + 2 = 5$, g) $6 \div 3 = 2$, h) $5 - 2 = 3$

9. an ordinal number 11. an even number
10. an odd number 12. a fraction

i) ten, j) one-tenth, k) tenth, l) eleven

Don't stop now! If you keep working you'll *heap up* a *pile* of new words!

VII. Put in the right noun.

1. I just bought a new ..... of gloves.
2. I need a ..... of scissors.
3. We write "2.3" and say "two ..... three."
4. You can't multiply if you don't know the ..... table.
5. "My father can't understand me. There's a generation ......"

VIII. Put in the right verb.

1. Six and three ..... nine. $(6 + 3 = 9)$
2. Six from nine ..... three. $(9 - 6 = 3)$
3. Two ..... into six three times. $(6 \div 2 = 3)$
4. Four ..... two ..... eight. $(4 \times 2 = 8)$
5. Four ..... by two ..... eight. $(4 \times 2 = 8)$
6. "No, something's wrong. The figures don't add up correctly. I must have ..... a mistake somewhere."
7. No, I don't need the whole loaf of bread; ..... it in two, please.
8. The river is too narrow for ships, so the government plans to ..... it.
9. I'm about to cook something. Won't you stay for a while and ..... a bite with us?

Have you realized that you have only a little more than a *dozen* questions left? *That's right!*

IX. Put in the right adjective, adverb or preposition.

1. Your expenses, my dear, are entirely out ..... proportion to our income.
2. He was driving ..... exactly 200 kilometres per hour.
3. Do you know how deep and how ..... the Rhine is at Bonn?
4. The ratio of boys to girls in the class is three ..... one.
5. It is not good to deprive a child ..... love.
6. The new teacher wants to fail half the class? That's going a bit ..... far!
7. He could fail 10% of the class ..... the most.

X. Review: Put in the right word.

1. One, three, five, seven, nine and eleven are ..... numbers.
2. Two, four, six, eight, ten, twelve are ..... numbers.
3. Your son just broke about half ..... dozen bottles.
4. Total ..... the bill, please.
5. I've been listening with only ..... an ear.
6. It's only ..... trifle. Don't worry about it.

Check your answers! How many *mistakes have you made?*

Key

I 1a, 2a, 3b, 4c

II 1c, 2c, 3a, 4b, 5b, 6a, 7b, 8c, 9c, 10a

III 1a, 2c, 3b, 4c, 5c, 6a, 7b, 8a (*Am* stories, *Br* storeys)

IV 1T, 2F, 3T, 4T, 5F, 6T, 7T, 8T

V 1e, 2c, 3a, 4b, 5d

VI 1d, 2a, 3c, 4b, 5f, 6h, 7e, 8g, 9k, 10l, 11i, 12j

VII 1 pair, 2 pair, 3 point, 4 multiplication, 5 gap

VIII 1 are (is), 2 leaves, 3 goes, 4 times ... are (is), 5 multiplied ... is, 6 made, 7 cut (divide, split), 8 widen (enlarge), 9 have

IX 1 of, 2 at, 3 wide, 4 to, 5 of, 6 too, 7 at

X 1 odd, 2 even, 3 a, 4 up, 5 half, 6 a

How many mistakes have you made?

	I to VI	VII to IX	X
Excellent	0— 2	0— 2	0 mistakes
Good	3— 4	3— 4	1 mistakes
Satisfactory	5— 7	5— 7	2 mistakes
Not very good	8—11	8—11	3 mistakes
Weak	over 11	over 11	over 3 mistakes

Are you *extremely* tired? If not, why don't you go on to the next chapter? Close the *gap* between your desires and your achievements!

Chapter II Time

There's no time like the *present* for learning English! So why *linger?* Let's start *instantly!*

I. What's the opposite?

1. Did they try to rob the bank *in broad daylight* or	a) in the afternoon? b) on a dark night? c) on a dark, narrow street?
2. Heracleitus wrote that nothing remains *constant;* everything	a) charges. b) changes. c) chains.
3. The professor said, "A man who *ceases* to think,	a) prefers to sleep." b) begins to sleep." c) yields to sleep."
4. Hope comes with the *dawn,* quiet with the	a) morning. b) dusk. c) night.

II. Which word or phrase has almost the same meaning?

1. I'll be there *in a flash!*	a) in a fast car b) in a police car c) very quickly
2. His answer was *instantaneous.*	a) He insisted on answering. b) He insisted his answer was right. c) He answered immediately.
3. She stood in the *twilight.*	a) light just after sunset b) light from the sun and a lamp c) light from coloured lamps
4. No work of man is *eternal.*	a) completely new b) truly repeatable c) able to last forever
5. Please be *on time.*	a) Come early. b) Come at the time we agreed on. c) Come a little late.
6. After the strike, the factory *resumed* production.	a) stopped b) started c) started again

7. He dreams of writing books for *posterity*.
   a) the people behind him
   b) the people born after him
   c) his own satisfaction

8. She worked for the *duration* of the war.
   a) until the war ended
   b) to help win the war
   c) to help delay the war

III. Which choice makes sense?

1. Take your time.
   a) And never come here again!
   b) I don't need your clock now.
   c) There's no hurry.

2. She lingered because
   a) the sunset was so beautiful.
   b) she wanted to leave.
   c) she was in a hurry.

3. He didn't arrive in time; he came
   a) on time.
   b) too late.
   c) punctually.

4. She left bright and early
   a) in the morning.
   b) at noon.
   c) the minute the sun came out.

5. He left for a period of
   a) a point.
   b) money.
   c) ten years.

6. Day and night cannot exist simultaneously but
   a) are real.
   b) must follow each other.
   c) also in autumn and winter.

7. He was born in the first decade of the
   a) month.
   b) year.
   c) century.

IV. Is it true or false?

	T	F
1. A wristwatch is more primitive than a sun-dial.	☐	☐
2. An alarm-clock rings and wakes you up in the morning.	☐	☐
3. The working-days are Monday to Friday.	☐	☐
4. The weekdays are Monday to Saturday.	☐	☐
5. A leap-year has only 364 days and comes once every two years.	☐	☐
6. Straw is more durable than steel.	☐	☐

V. Find the nouns which go together.

1. eternity
2. calendar
3. twilight
4. wrist
5. alarm

a) months, b) watch, c) clock, d) evening, e) endlessness

VI. Find the words which go together.

1. in an .....
2. in a .....
3. in .....
4. in broad .....
5. to set a .....
6. at .....

a) time, b) instant, c) flash, d) watch, e) noon, f) daylight

7. constant
8. primitive
9. previously
10. instantly
11. present

g) simple, h) current, i) immediately, j) earlier, k) unchanging

Now you can relax for a minute. *Take your time; there's no hurry.* By the way, *what do you do in your spare time?* Do you read English books and newspapers? If you do, then *one of these days* you'll discover to your own surprise that you can think in English.

Come on — the pause is over. Time to *resume* work!

VII. Put in the right noun.

1. You were born 20 years ago today? So today's your .....! Well, happy .....!
2. Man passes from birth to childhood, youth, middle age, old ..... and then to death.
3. The sun rises at dawn and sets at .....
4. Ten in the morning is 10 a.m. Ten in the evening is 10 .....
5. Fifteen minutes is a ..... of an hour.
6. Thirty minutes is ..... an hour.

VIII. Put in the right verb.

1. It must be eleven; I just heard the clock ..... eleven.
2. My watch is an hour fast. I'll have to ..... it back an hour.
3. What do you ..... in your spare time?
4. There's no rush. It can ..... until tomorrow.
5. So long! ..... you again!

IX. Put in the right adjective, adverb or preposition.

1. The poor girl works 12 hours a day, from morning ..... night.
2. I don't know when, but one ..... these days, I'm going to leave.
3. Today is December 25th. ..... Christmas!
4. Today is January 1st. ..... New Year!
5. Today is the 5th ..... February.
6. Today is Wednesday. Monday was the day ..... yesterday, and Friday is the day ..... tomorrow.
7. He's leaving the middle ..... next week and will be gone ..... a few days.
8. I waited a whole hour ..... you.
9. If you have to get up so early, set the alarm ..... five o'clock in the morning.
10. What's the time? ..... my watch it's five-thirty.
11. We eat ..... noon.
12. Is he coming in the morning, ... the afternoon, ... the evening or ..... night?
13. He said he would come in less than half a minute, and he really was here ..... an instant.
14. We get the same old food, day in, day .....
15. "Ten minutes ..... eleven" means 11:10.
16. "Ten minutes ..... eleven" means 10:50.
17. "A quarter ..... eleven" means 11:15.
18. "A quarter ..... eleven" means 10:45.

X. Review: Put in the right word.

1. Fifteen minutes is a .... hour.
2. Thirty minutes is .... hour.
3. I'm certain my watch is right. I ..... it when the radio gave the time.
4. We'll start driving bright and ..... tomorrow.
5. A ..... lists the days, weeks and months of a year.

Time to *cease* work and check your answers!

Key

I 1b, 2b, 3b, 4b

II 1c, 2c, 3a, 4c, 5b, 6c, 7b, 8a

III 1c, 2a, 3b, 4a, 5c, 6b, 7c

IV 1F, 2T, 3T, 4T, 5F, 6F

V 1e, 2a, 3d, 4b, 5c

VI 1b, 2c, 3a, 4f, 5d, 6e, 7k, 8g, 9j, 10i, 11h

VII 1 birthday ... birthday, 2 age, 3 dusk (sunset), 4 p.m., 5 quarter, 6 half

VIII 1 strike, 2 set (put, turn), 3 do, 4 wait, 5 See

IX 1 till (to), 2 of, 3 Merry, 4 Happy, 5 of, 6 before ... after, 7 of ... for, 8 for, 9 for, 10 By (According to), 11 at, 12 in ... in ... at, 13 in, 14 out, 15 past, 16 to, 17 past, 18 to

X 1 quarter of an, 2 half an, 3 set (checked), 4 early, 5 calendar

How many mistakes have you made?

	I to VI	VII to IX	X
Excellent	0— 2	0— 3	0 mistakes
Good	3— 4	4— 6	1 mistakes
Satisfactory	5— 7	7—10	2 mistakes
Not very good	8—11	11—15	3 mistakes
Weak	over 11	over 15	over 3 mistakes

Are you ready to let some time *elapse* before the next lesson? Do you want to say, "Oh, *it can wait until tomorrow*"? Well, let's think it over!

Learning a language takes *constant* practice, *day in, day out.* You can't learn it in an *instant!*

What's the time? Is it still *bright and early?* Or has *twilight* already come? Take a look at your *wristwatch.* If you're not too tired, *put your watch back* one hour, pretend you have an extra hour, and start the next lesson!

Chapter III The Universe

Is the *thermometer* falling? Does the *barometer* show that a *thunderstorm* is coming? Is the wind *howling* outside, and will you get *soaked to the skin* if you step outside? Wonderful! Then you can stay inside and practise English! Let's hope *the weather keeps up!*

Or *is the sun shining? Has a breeze sprung up?* That's even better! *In fine weather* you can read English *in the open air*. Take your book out into the garden or out to the *pasture*, if there's one near you, and when you've finished this book, *you'll speak excellent English!*

I. What's the opposite?

1. Is the moon *waxing* tonight or
   a) bright?
   b) soft?
   c) waning?

2. Australia is *spacious;* Singapore is
   a) a small island.
   b) full of smoke.
   c) small and crowded.

3. These yellow flowers are *widespread*, but these white ones are
   a) not yet in bloom.
   b) the right size.
   c) limited to this area.

4. Do you think it'll be *overcast* tomorrow, or
   a) a windless day?
   b) a clear day?
   c) a day without sunshine?

5. My car works better on *chilly* days than on
   a) warm days.
   b) cool days.
   c) cold days.

6. Steam is almost *invisible*, but black smoke is
   a) easily seen.
   b) outlined.
   c) out of view.

7. I'd rather swim in a *shallow* river than in a
   a) deep one.
   b) dirty one.
   c) dangerous one.

8. Some lakes are *muddy*, others are
   a) deep.
   b) clear.
   c) quiet.

II. Which word or phrase has almost the same meaning?

1. What a *damp* day! The air feels so
   a) moist.
   b) unpleasant.
   c) hot, wet and steamy.
2. The radio said *stormy* weather tomorrow.
   a) changeable
   b) windy
   c) rainy and windy
3. Is it *thawing?*
   a) Is it snowing?
   b) Is the water freezing?
   c) Is the ice melting?
4. What a *cloudburst!*
   a) sudden, violent rain
   b) sudden appearance of clouds
   c) sudden disappearance of clouds
5. *It's raining cats and dogs.*
   a) The road is wet from cats and dogs.
   b) It's raining slightly.
   c) It's raining very hard.
6. *It looks like rain.*
   a) I think it's going to rain.
   b) I think it's raining.
   c) I think it was raining.
7. There's a heavy *mist* outside.
   a) air pressure
   b) dirt in the air
   c) tiny drops of water in the air
8. A *heat wave* is coming!
   a) air from a desert
   b) many days of hot weather
   c) warm water in the ocean
9. We've never had such a *cold spell!*
   a) very cold weather for a while
   b) unfriendly greeting
   c) evil spell
10. Run for the house! A *thunderstorm* is coming!
    a) thunder
    b) thunder and lightning
    c) rain, wind, thunder and lightning
11. There's a lot of *moisture* in the air.
    a) dirt
    b) smoke
    c) wetness
12. I hope *the weather keeps up.*
    a) it doesn't rain
    b) the clouds go away
    c) the weather continues as it is

13. It's so *sultry* today; I don't want to do anything!
   a) hot
   b) hot, damp and heavy
   c) unpredictable

14. What *foul weather!*
   a) weather for playing football
   b) rainy, windy, unpleasant
   c) the sky is full of clouds

15. We're entering the biggest *lock.*
   a) part of a canal
   b) lake in Scotland
   c) hole in the earth

16. *It's blowing a gale!*
   a) I'm very angry!
   b) The ship is sinking!
   c) The wind is very strong!

17. I can't *bear* this heat.
   a) I can't carry this thing.
   b) It's too hot for me.
   c) Bears like cool weather.

18. The water *burst forth* from the rock.
   a) suddenly came pouring out of
   b) fell violently onto
   c) was lying on

19. *Between you and me,* he acts like a fool.
   a) compared to you and me
   b) whenever he's with us
   c) don't tell anyone I said this

20. I see her *now and then.*
   a) now and sometime in the future
   b) now and sometime in the past
   c) once in a while

21. The *expanse* of countryside was glorious!
   a) cloudless sky
   b) very wide area
   c) expensive way of life

22. He wants to *expand* his farm.
   a) explain it to us
   b) make it larger
   c) sell it

23. He has an *extensive* farm.
   a) large
   b) unusual
   c) expensive

24. The entire *neighbourhood* was destroyed by fire.
   a) the buildings in a small area
   b) the countryside
   c) the hats of the neighbours

25. The *remoteness* of the stars astonished him.
a) silent beauty
b) movement in a great circle
c) great distance and strangeness

26. Is the package too *bulky* to be sent by mail?
a) large
b) heavy
c) poorly wrapped

27. He sent us a *voluminous* report.
a) large
b) printed
c) ready to be printed

28. Be careful in the *marsh!*
a) month after February
b) low wet ground
c) line of walking soldiers

29. She gave a *comprehensive* answer.
a) very common
b) very complete
c) very comfortable

30. We're *centrally located.*
a) in the centre of the building
b) in the middle of town
c) in the local telephone book

III. Which choice makes sense?

1. The lake was overflowing
a) after the heavy rains.
b) because the water was so dirty.
c) so we went sailing.

2. I'm shivering
a) this secret message.
b) the boat to England.
c) because it's cold here.

3. "What's howling out there?"
a) "The birds."
b) "The wind."
c) "The thunder."

4. What a raging
a) tower!
b) coast!
c) storm!

5. Don't splash me with that
a) water!
b) coal!
c) dust!

6. The water was trickling
a) high into the air.
b) through the pipes.
c) down the powerful river.

7. When an area is hit by drought,
a) snow covers everything.
b) the land dries up.
c) the rivers and lakes overflow.

8. I just felt a raindrop.
a) It's going to rain.
b) It'll stop raining soon.
c) And it hurt.

9. I love to look at the dew
a) in the morning.
b) in the afternoon.
c) of children.

10. "What does the weather forecast say?"
a) "It was hot."
b) "It's hot."
c) "It will be hot."

11. "How did you get so sunburnt?"
a) "I was on the beach yesterday."
b) "I was too close to the fire."
c) "From my son."

12. There's a ford ahead! We can
a) cross the river there.
b) ride in it.
c) ask for help there.

13. The tides are influenced by
a) the water.
b) the ropes.
c) the moon.

14. Which cliff
a) did you climb up?
b) did he swim in?
c) flew away?

15. The soldiers were outlined against
a) the attack.
b) the enemy.
c) the sky.

16. The dimensions of the room are
a) 22° to 26° Centigrade.
b) bright yellow and soft brown.
c) in metres, five by five by three.

17. The bird soared
a) with his feet.
b) up into the air.
c) with his feathers.

18. The bird descended
a) in the nest.
b) into the air.
c) to the treetop.

IV. Is it true or false?

		T	F
1.	Africa is a continent.	☐	☐
2.	England is part of the mainland of Europe.	☐	☐
3.	The Rhine has its source in the Netherlands.	☐	☐
4.	It's a hazy day if there is a very light fog.	☐	☐
5.	It's never foggy in London.	☐	☐
6.	A blazing sun is a sun behind clouds.	☐	☐
7.	An eclipse of the sun can bring darkness at noon.	☐	☐
8.	The earth and the sun are planets.	☐	☐
9.	The earth revolves around the sun.	☐	☐
10.	If hail hits you, it can hurt.	☐	☐
11.	A barometer measures the atmospheric pressure.	☐	☐
12.	A thermometer measures water pressure.	☐	☐
13.	A hurricane is an old woman who can usually forecast the weather.	☐	☐
14.	A plateau is a mountain area with many ridges and passes.	☐	☐
15.	A steep hill is a hill which has steps cut into it.	☐	☐
16.	A vacuum is a space without air.	☐	☐
17.	Men and women are extinct.	☐	☐
18.	A boulder is a person who is bold.	☐	☐
19.	A frontier is a man who guards a house.	☐	☐
20.	There is a boundary between China and the USSR.	☐	☐
21.	An isthmus connects two larger pieces of land.	☐	☐

V. Find the nouns which go together.

1. brook
2. inundation
3. breakers
4. whirlpool
5. glacier

a) stream, b) ice, c) eddy, d) flood, e) waves

6. snowstorm
7. ford
8. watershed
9. beach
10. volcano

f) crossing, g) eruption, h) snowflake, i) divide, j) sand

11. sunbeam
12. pasture
13. oasis
14. highlands
15. boulder
16. extremity

k) mountains, l) rock, m) end, n) sunshine, o) desert, p) grass

VI. Find the words which go together.

1. atmospheric ..... 3. heat .....
2. weather ..... 4. cold .....

a) spell, b) forecast, c) pressure, d) wave

5. high ..... 7. shooting ..... 9. South .....
6. new ..... 8. milky .....

e) star, f) tide, g) Pole, h) moon, i) way

10. the ice ..... 12. lightning .....
11. the sun ..... 13. the stars .....

j) twinkle, k) strikes, l) shines, m) thaws

VII. Put in the right noun.

1. Bonn is the capital of West .....
2. Vienna is the capital of .....
3. Zurich is the largest city in .....
4. The English ..... is the stretch of water between England and France.
5. The water between Norway, England and Denmark is called the .....
6. The water between Spain and Greece is called the .....
7. The ocean between Europe and America is called the .....
8. We travelled from Sweden to Italy, from north to .....
9. San Francisco was destroyed in 1906 by an ....., when the earth shook violently.
10. Men dig mines, but a large hole made by nature is a .....
11. The government built a ..... across the river to hold back the water.

When you began to learn English you were *at the foot of the mountain*. Now you're near the *summit*. Maybe the road up was sometimes *steep*, but think of the *far-reaching* advantages your *extensive* knowledge of English will bring! You'll add a new world, a new *dimension* to your experiences! But don't slow down now! Keep on working!

VIII. Put in the right verb.

1. The Moselle ..... into the Rhine at Coblenz.
2. The United States ..... north of Mexico.
3. The Soviet Union ..... east of Poland.
4. The Netherlands ..... north of Belgium.
5. The Alps ..... famous for winter sports.

IX. Put in the right adjective, adverb or preposition.

1. Did Peary go to the South Pole or the ..... Pole?
2. The Zugspitze is 2,966 metres ..... sea-level.
3. I was caught in the rain yesterday, and got soaked ..... the skin.
4. The sky is clearing .....
5. It's 30 degrees ..... the shade.
6. When we went camping, we slept out ..... doors.
7. I love to sleep ..... the open air when I go camping.
8. Before she accepted him, she looked him ..... from head to foot.
9. I didn't lose it — it must be here somewhere, but I can't lay my hands ..... it right now.
10. Now we know why they did it! Now we're ..... the bottom of the problem!
11. Say it ..... English, please.
12. The book was translated ..... English.
13. We live directly above him; he lives one floor ..... us.
14. It's not far; it's only a few steps ..... here.

X. Review: Put in the right word.

1. If the weather keeps ....., we can go swimming tomorrow.
2. It looks ..... rain.
3. It's raining cats and .....
4. On a clear night you can see the stars of the milky .....
5. It's going to rain tomorrow. I just heard the weather ..... on the radio.
6. My son was so excited that the words simply ..... forth from him.

Did you *write excellent English?* Here are the answers for you!

Key

I 1c, 2c, 3c, 4b, 5a, 6a, 7a, 8b

II 1a, 2c, 3c, 4a, 5c, 6a, 7c, 8b, 9a, 10c, 11c, 12c, 13b, 14b, 15a, 16c, 17b, 18a, 19c, 20c, 21b, 22b, 23a, 24a, 25c, 26a, 27a, 28b, 29b, 30b

III 1a, 2c, 3b, 4c, 5a, 6b, 7b, 8a, 9a, 10c, 11a, 12a, 13c, 14a, 15c, 16c, 17b, 18c

IV 1T, 2F, 3F, 4T, 5F, 6F, 7T, 8F, 9T, 10T, 11T, 12F, 13F, 14F, 15F, 16T, 17F, 18F, 19F, 20T, 21T

V 1a, 2d, 3e, 4c, 5b, 6h, 7f, 8i, 9j, 10g, 11n, 12p, 13o, 14k, 15l, 16m

VI 1c, 2b, 3d, 4a, 5f, 6h, 7e, 8i, 9g, 10m, 11l, 12k, 13j

VII 1 Germany, 2 Austria, 3 Switzerland, 4 Channel, 5 North Sea, 6 Mediterranean, 7 Atlantic Ocean, 8 south, 9 earthquake, 10 cave, 11 dam

VIII 1 flows, 2 is, 3 is, 4 are, 5 are

IX 1 North, 2 above, 3 to, 4 up, 5 in, 6 of, 7 in, 8 over, 9 on, 10 at, 11 in, 12 into (from), 13 below, 14 from

X 1 up, 2 like, 3 dogs, 4 way, 5 forecast, 6 burst

How many mistakes have you made?

	I to VI	VII to IX	X
Excellent	0— 5	0— 3	0 mistakes
Good	6—10	4— 6	1 mistakes
Satisfactory	11—17	7—10	2 mistakes
Not very good	18—26	11—16	3 mistakes
Weak	over 26	over 16	over 3 mistakes

Have some *English* people or some *Americans* moved into the *neighbourhood?* Or maybe some *Irish*, *Scottish*, or *Welsh* people, or some *Australians?* Go and speak to them in English! And did you know that most *Africans* and *Asians* living in *Europe* speak English? You've had a chance to *lay the foundations* for a solid knowledge of the language; you can make use of it *now and then*. But prepare yourself by looking at the next chapter. You'll be *dazzled* when you see how quickly you can do it!

Chapter IV Man

Do your friends say that you *have no feeling* for languages? *Don't listen to them! We'll tell you something in confidence:* learning a foreign language is simply a matter of repetition. That's all. That's the big secret. Of course, some people may have to repeat their exercises more often than others, but this is no reason for you to *mourn!* You can have fun no matter how often you repeat an exercise!

I. What's the opposite?

1. My sister's hair is full of *curls*, but mine is very
   a) straight.
   b) dry.
   c) clean.

2. She was *all smiles* when she heard that her former husband was
   a) sad.
   b) lazy.
   c) tired.

3. Careful! That chair is *wobbly*. Come and sit on this
   a) dry chair.
   b) comfortable chair.
   c) firm chair.

4. She gave him a *furtive* look, not
   a) a shy, friendly look.
   b) an open, bold look.
   c) a secret, hidden look.

5. I'm reading, so please *keep quiet!* Don't
   a) make so much noise.
   b) move the desk.
   c) come into my room.

6. This bread is *delicious*, but those cheeses
   a) look terrible.
   b) taste terrible.
   c) smell terrible.

7. He had a *relapse*, though the doctor had expected he
   a) would recover.
   b) wouldn't faint.
   c) wouldn't eat anything.

II. Which word or phrase has almost the same meaning?

1. The cowboy was *lanky*.
   a) tall and thin
   b) short and fat
   c) full of courage

2. What a *striking* girl!
   a) She is a hard union leader.
   b) She hits people when she's angry.
   c) She is a girl people notice.

3. Oh! — Sorry! Did I kick you in the *shin?*
   a) front of the lower leg
   b) knee
   c) toes

4. Ow! I bit the *tip* of my tongue!
   a) front part
   b) left side
   c) right side

5. He *gazed* at the stars in wonder.
   a) thought about them
   b) tried to count them
   c) looked at them for a long time

6. She's very *plump.*
   a) short, thick and strong
   b) thin, hard and tough
   c) round and soft

7. My uncle is small and *stout.*
   a) rather fat
   b) thin, hard and tough
   c) clever, bold and active

8. The diplomat *conducted himself well.*
   a) worked with great energy and speed
   b) made everyone around him happy
   c) acted calmly and honourably

9. The farmers here need *sturdy* bodies.
   a) large
   b) brown from the sun
   c) strong, solid

10. The farmers' wives are *robust.*
    a) fat
    b) red-brown from the sun
    c) strong, healthy, full of energy

11. He's 80 years old but still has a *vigorous* mind.
    a) open to new things, curious
    b) alert, lively, active and strong
    c) simple, honest, pure and sincere

12. He's such a poor, *sickly* fellow.
    a) thin
    b) weak and often ill
    c) stupid

13. She didn't see her father, but she *sensed* he was there.
    a) expected
    b) felt
    c) knew

14. It was absolutely *deafening* at the railway station!
    a) very dangerous
    b) full of thieves
    c) extremely loud

15. He *committed suicide.*
   a) He killed himself.
   b) He killed someone.
   c) He went to the hospital.

16. That's quite a *fracture* he has!
   a) bloody arm or leg
   b) broken bone
   c) machine for doctors

17. She had a splitting *headache.*
   a) Her head was cut open.
   b) Her head hurt very much.
   c) She split a large oak tree.

18. My doctor *consulted* another doctor.
   a) asked for advice
   b) blamed
   c) got money from

19. Is it a *hereditary* disease?
   a) contageous
   b) dangerous
   c) passed on from parent to child

20. I'm *exhausted!*
   a) out of breath
   b) out of energy
   c) out of patience

21. The weather was *dismal.*
   a) dark, cold, rainy, unfriendly
   b) warm, sunny, friendly
   c) unusual for the season

22. The doctor told him he'll be *crippled* for life. He'll
   a) never walk again.
   b) never talk again.
   c) never see again.

23. He has been *confined to his bed.*
   a) He can't get out of bed.
   b) He refuses to get out of bed.
   c) He isn't allowed to get out of bed.

24. My feet are *swelling up!*
   a) becoming larger
   b) becoming lighter and thinner
   c) becoming red

25. She has a beautiful *complexion.*
   a) clothes
   b) figure
   c) colour in her face

26. He's *deceased.*
   a) He has a serious disease.
   b) He cut himself badly.
   c) He's dead.

We never said we would offer you a *meagre* selection of questions!

III. Which choice makes sense?

1. He grew pale after he
   a) bought enough seeds.
   b) began to eat good food.
   c) heard his mother had died.

2. The girl made a sour face, and we knew
   a) she was tired.
   b) she didn't like the food.
   c) her face had been burned.

3. He winked at her with
   a) one eye.
   b) a flag.
   c) his hand.

4. After being in the dark room, he blinked when he
   a) hit the wall.
   b) stepped on the cat.
   c) came into the bright sunlight.

5. He yawned because he was
   a) drowsy.
   b) polite.
   c) drowning.

6. Chin up!
   a) Don't be discouraged.
   b) I want to take a photo of you.
   c) You look tired.

7. He shrugged his shoulders to tell us that
   a) his back hurt.
   b) he couldn't see it.
   c) he didn't care about it.

8. The policeman made a sign to me, so I
   a) signed it.
   b) went to him.
   c) shot him.

9. He gave me such a piercing look that I felt he was
   a) about to hit me.
   b) looking right through me.
   c) looking at someone behind me.

10. What a disagreeable person!
    a) Everyone always laughs at him.
    b) I never want to see him again.
    c) I hope he comes back soon.

11. The doctor vaccinated him
    a) with fresh blood.
    b) against polio.
    c) and removed it a week later.

12. Would you like to take a nap
    a) of whisky?
    b) for your wife?
    c) this afternoon?

13. "I'm afraid you'll have to undergo an operation,"
a) the general told his officers.
b) the doctor told his patient.
c) the bank manager told the doctor.

14. He lost consciousness and
a) found it in the hospital.
b) married her.
c) woke up several hours later.

15. A person who is deaf and dumb can neither
a) hear nor work with his hands.
b) speak nor think.
c) hear nor speak.

16. "I'm dizzy! Let me
a) stand up."
b) sit down."
c) get dressed."

17. The boy drowned
a) in the river.
b) on land.
c) in the air.

18. He gave her a quick glance
a) and it jumped away from her.
b) and she paid him for it.
c) and she looked back at him.

19. The poor old man stuttered so much that we
a) helped him put on his coat.
b) rushed him to a doctor.
c) couldn't understand him.

20. If you're going to snore,
a) go and beg from him. He's rich.
b) you'll need more string.
c) I'll sleep in the other room.

21. Why are you limping? Is there something wrong with your
a) arm?
b) leg?
c) eyes?

22. If he has patients, then he must be
a) a patient man.
b) a man of patience.
c) a doctor or dentist.

23. Was she born blind or
a) did she lose her sight as a child?
b) can her baby see normally?
c) is she totally blind?

24. Is your hearing good or are you
a) hearing evil?
b) hard of hearing?
c) here and there?

25. She's as graceful as a
a) dog eating grass.
b) cat.
c) grocer.

26. The nurses disinfected
a) the hospital room.
b) the insects.
c) the infection.

Is the sweat running down your forehead yet? No? Then go on to the next exercise!

IV. Is it true or false?

	T	F
1. The brain is a part of the nervous system.	☐	☐
2. The vocal chords are in the throat and produce sounds.	☐	☐
3. Most young women nowadays want to have a small waist.	☐	☐
4. The abdomen consists mainly of the stomach and the bowels.	☐	☐
5. The belly consists mainly of the stomach and the bowels.	☐	☐
6. The thigh is below the ankle.	☐	☐
7. People perspire most in cold weather.	☐	☐
8. People weep when they are very unhappy.	☐	☐
9. A group of little boys can be very noisy.	☐	☐
10. Sound travels by sound waves.	☐	☐
11. Sunstroke is a sudden appearance of the sun.	☐	☐
12. A person who is feeble-minded is usually very clever.	☐	☐
13. A person who is unconscious can fix a broken radio.	☐	☐
14. Flu is a contagious disease.	☐	☐
15. Tuberculosis is a heart disease.	☐	☐
16. A person who has had polio may have to limp.	☐	☐
17. Cancer is never malignant.	☐	☐
18. A person who is making a good recovery is catching a disease for the second time.	☐	☐
19. Measles is a disease which spreads by infection.	☐	☐
20. After a stomach ulcer has healed, it bleeds.	☐	☐
21. A remedy for a disease can be a pill, an ointment or an injection.	☐	☐
22. Doctors and nurses often have night-duty.	☐	☐
23. A corpse is put into a coffin.	☐	☐

Some of these questions may seem *gloomy* and *dismal;* the title of this chapter is "Man", and that includes *mortality*. Let's face it: sometimes life is *disagreeable*. We hope we don't give you an *upset stomach*, or make you *grow pale*. But don't worry; you'll *recover* as soon as you discover how many new words you've learned!

V. Find the nouns which go together.

1. windpipe
2. complexion
3. knuckle
4. pulse
5. skull
6. spine
7. forearm

a) backbone, b) blood, c) breath, d) face, e) upper arm, f) finger, g) head

8. fracture
9. illness
10. gravestone
11. cremation

h) epitaph, i) injury, j) sickness, k) urn

VI. Find the words which go together.

1. he ..... his ankle
2. he had his tonsils .....
3. he ..... his head
4. his appendix .....
5. he ..... through his nose

a) raised, b) removed, c) sprained, d) talks, e) burst

6. to have a rapid .....
7. to be hard of .....
8. to shed .....
9. to make a sour .....
10. to make ..... at someone

f) faces, g) face, h) pulse, i) tears, j) hearing

11. polio
12. pneumonia
13. measles
14. cancer

k) a growth, l) small red spots, m) lungs, n) arms or legs

15. insane
16. mute
17. drowsy
18. furtive

o) sleepy, p) secret, q) dumb, r) mad

How are you? Are you still *wide-awake?* Or did those last exercises leave you *panting*, or even *gasping* for breath? *Are you drowsy? Yawning?* Don't work to the point of *exhaustion!* We don't want you to have a *breakdown* or a *collapse!* Do you feel *dizzy?* If you're *exhausted*, stop for a while and *take a nap*, but come back to these exercises as soon as you feel *vigorous* again!

VII. Put in the right noun.

1. When you meet someone, you shake ..... with him.
2. In the dark, the ..... of the eye becomes larger, and in bright light it becomes smaller.
3. He didn't want to wake up his wife, so he walked very quietly, on .....
4. The old lady said she could tell me my future by looking at the lines on the ..... of my hand.
5. The names of the five fingers are: ....., first finger, middle finger, ring finger and little finger.
6. The five senses are: sight, smell, taste, ... and .....
7. The pulse tells how fast the ..... beats.
8. The doctor said to take the pills three ..... daily after meals.
9. The doctor gave me an .....; he stuck a long needle into me, and it still hurts.
10. He was so badly hurt in the car accident that he needed a ..... transfusion.
11. He's growing old, and his ..... is getting grey.
12. She died three days ago, and the ..... will be tomorrow.
13. The place where people are buried is called a .....
14. They put a very simple ..... on his grave, giving only his name, date of birth, and date of death.
15. They placed a beautiful, round ..... of green leaves on the grave.

VIII. Put in the right verb.

1. She agreed with me, so she ..... her head.
2. She disagreed with me, so she ..... her head.
3. It was so hot that the sweat ..... down his forehead.
4. All I do is worry, worry, worry about you. Are you trying to ..... a nail into my coffin?
5. I feel so weak. I seem to have ..... all my strength.
6. I don't think the new doctor is very good. He didn't even ..... my pulse.
7. He needs glasses because his sight ..... very poor.
8. She's sick. She ..... a sore throat.
9. He ..... a temperature today, so he's staying in bed.
10. I can't go to work today; I have to ..... a funeral.
11. The plane flew by so fast that I only ..... a glimpse of it.
12. Under every window in the train was this sign: "Do not ..... out of the window!"

Do you feel hungry? Wait a minute! Don't leave the last two exercises *dangling!* Finish them, and then you can check your answers, stop, and have a *delicious* meal!

IX. Put in the right adjective, adverb or preposition.

1. I feel absolutely wonderful! I'm ..... the best of health!
2. He's healthy, happy, and in the prime ..... life.
3. I can't do the work. It's too much ..... me.
4. I must speak to him! It's a matter ..... life and death.
5. My hair stood ..... end when I saw the dead man move his eyes.
6. I didn't ask you for advice! Don't stick your nose ..... other people's business!
7. We must be near a fish-shop; it smells ..... fish here.
8. When the car hit me, I felt a sharp pain ..... my head.
9. Please speak louder. I'm ..... in one ear.
10. "Your lip is all sore." — "Which one? The upper lip or the ..... lip?"
11. Within three days he recovered ..... the disease.
12. "How are you?" — "Not too bad, not too good. So, ..."
13. His mother complained sadly, "My son doesn't listen ..... me."
14. He built the house by himself, by the sweat ..... his brow.
15. A husky, robust man is not at all feminine; he's very .....
16. Of course you can't talk to him about music! He has absolutely no feeling ..... music.
17. The baby weighed eight pounds ..... birth.

X. Review: Put in the right word.

1. When the older brother is reading, the younger brother must keep .....
2. He didn't want to wake ..... his wife, so he walked very quietly.
3. She was ..... smiles.
4. The ..... chords are in the throat.
5. My foot is swelling .....
6. She ..... a sour face.
7. He's been confined ..... his bed.

Time to *consult* the answer-key!

Key

I 1a, 2a, 3c, 4b, 5a, 6b, 7a

II 1a, 2c, 3a, 4a, 5c, 6c, 7a, 8c, 9c, 10c, 11b, 12b, 13b, 14c, 15a, 16b, 17b, 18a, 19c, 20b, 21a, 22a, 23c, 24a, 25c, 26c

III 1c, 2b, 3a, 4c, 5a, 6a, 7c, 8b, 9b, 10b, 11b, 12c, 13b, 14c, 15c, 16b, 17a, 18c, 19c, 20c, 21b, 22c, 23a, 24b, 25b, 26a

IV 1T, 2T, 3T, 4T, 5T, 6F, 7F, 8T, 9T, 10T, 11F, 12F, 13F, 14T, 15F, 16T, 17F, 18F, 19T, 20F, 21T, 22T, 23T

V 1c, 2d, 3f, 4b, 5g, 6a, 7e, 8i, 9j, 10h, 11k

VI 1c, 2b, 3a, 4e, 5d, 6h, 7j, 8i, 9g, 10f, 11n, 12m, 13l, 14k, 15r, 16q, 17o, 18p

VII 1 hands, 2 pupil, 3 tiptoe, 4 palm, 5 thumb, 6 hearing ... touch, 7 heart, 8 times, 9 injection, 10 blood, 11 hair, 12 funeral (burial), 13 cemetery (graveyard), 14 gravestone (stone, epitaph), 15 wreath

VIII 1 nodded, 2 shook, 3 ran, 4 drive, 5 lost, 6 feel (check, take), 7 is, 8 has, 9 has, 10 attend (go to), 11 caught (had, got), 12 lean

IX 1 in, 2 of, 3 for, 4 of, 5 on, 6 into, 7 of, 8 in, 9 deaf, 10 lower, 11 from, 12 so, 13 to, 14 of, 15 masculine, 16 for, 17 at

X 1 quiet, 2 up, 3 all, 4 vocal, 5 up, 6 made, 7 to

How many mistakes have you made?

	I to VI	VII to IX	X
Excellent	0—5	0—4	0 mistakes
Good	6—11	5—8	1 mistakes
Satisfactory	12—18	9—14	2 mistakes
Not very good	19—28	15—22	3 mistakes
Weak	over 28	over 22	over 3 mistakes

Did you make too many mistakes? It doesn't help to *shrug your shoulders*, *make a sour face*, or be *down in the mouth*. *Chin up!* Go back and do the difficult questions again!

Or did you make very few mistakes? Are you *all smiles?* Wonderful! The next chapter is waiting for you!

Chapter V The Soul and the Mind

Part 1: Emotions, Virtues and Vices

You don't have to *make any* painful *sacrifices* to learn English! All you need is *enthusiasm*, *resolution* and *cheerfulness!*

What's the secret of staying in a good *frame of mind* while learning? We'll tell you: whenever you make mistakes, don't get *upset*, and don't *give vent to your feelings*. Be *tolerant*, *good-natured*, ready to laugh.

I. What's the opposite?

1. "Doctor, my problem is, whenever my wife feels *courageous*, I feel quite
   a) alone."
   b) unfriendly."
   c) cowardly."
2. An *impudent* child can be more fun than a
   a) brave one.
   b) respectful one.
   c) careful one.
3. "You're a fool for wanting to marry that *extravagant* woman! A man needs a
   a) thrifty wife."
   b) natural wife."
   c) relaxed, calm wife."
4. You're too *self-conscious!*
   a) Just relax and be natural!
   b) Forget about your conscience!
   c) Don't be so sure of yourself!
5. Be a little more *discreet!* Don't be so
   a) shy!
   b) outspoken!
   c) prejudiced!
6. "She's such a *haughty* creature! She never tries to
   a) be humble."
   b) be honest."
   c) behave herself."
7. Some political leaders are *honourable*, others
   a) are base.
   b) honour nobody.
   c) are forgotten.
8. Why do you *rely on* him when you know you should
   a) forgive him?
   b) forget him?
   c) mistrust him?
9. Your *impatience* is terrible!
   a) You need more patients.
   b) You should be more patient.
   c) You should be out of patience.

10. Although I *disapprove* of her idea, I'll be glad to
   a) prove his.
   b) give you proof of his.
   c) approve his.

11. An *unjust* man is usually less respected than one who
   a) is on time.
   b) justifies himself.
   c) is fair.

12. Are *selfish* people as happy as
   a) normal people ?
   b) people who don't sell fish ?
   c) unselfish people ?

13. She left her *cautious* boyfriend as soon as she found
   a) a rich one.
   b) a bold one.
   c) a strong one.

14. The President wants to use *moderation* rather than
   a) old methods.
   b) weak measures.
   c) extreme measures.

15. She *fascinates* me, but I suppose I
   a) bore her.
   b) amuse her.
   c) astonish her.

16. She's always so *passionate!* I've never seen her
   a) excited.
   b) active.
   c) calm and composed.

17. "Strange, isn't it ? The most *talkative* girl I know married a man who
   a) is very reserved."
   b) speaks very well."
   c) speaks very softly."

18. Life is full of *grief* and
   a) giving.
   b) joy.
   c) jealousy.

19. Why did he *scold* me and
   a) praise her ?
   b) doubt her ?
   c) discourage her ?

20. He *scorns* you only because his wife
   a) admires you.
   b) complains about you.
   c) tries to protect you.

21. Don't be so *gloomy*. Try to be
   a) peaceful.
   b) cheerful.
   c) humble.

22. In the mornings I'm *irritable*, but in the evenings
   a) I'm off the table.
   b) I'm relaxed and tolerant.
   c) I make a lot of mistakes.

23. *Affectionate* mothers rarely have children who are
a) natural.
b) cold.
c) unable to affect people.

24. I don't believe you when you say you're *indifferent*. I think you
a) are different.
b) know the difference.
c) care about it.

25. It's a story of *vice* and
a) verse.
b) virtue.
c) presidents.

26. He gives the impression of being *self-confident*, but he really
a) can't keep a secret.
b) is unsure of himself.
c) is gentle.

Here's a poem, to show the meaning of *thoughtful*. You only need to know that "to chew" means "to crush food between your teeth while eating":

A gum-chewing girl and a grass-chewing cow:
I know there's a difference, somewhere, somehow.
Ah yes! I think I have it now:
There's a *thoughtful* look on the face of the cow.

II. Which word or phrase has almost the same meaning?

1. I respect his *sincerity*.
a) honesty
b) efficiency
c) sacrifice

2. She likes *affection*.
a) She likes to pretend.
b) She likes to affect people.
c) She likes to be loved.

3. What an *outspoken*, clever fellow!
a) He's unusually clever.
b) Everybody says that he's clever.
c) He says what he thinks.

4. A *conscientious* worker
a) likes his work.
b) does careful, honest work.
c) works well with others.

5. She has a cheerful *disposition*.
a) She just got a lot of money.
b) She likes to make us cheerful.
c) She's usually cheerful.

6. A *venerable* old man
   a) chases young girls.
   b) is defenceless.
   c) is highly respected.

7. His father was a *fearless* soldier.
   a) without fear
   b) fearful
   c) feared by the enemy

8. I like him because of his *humility;*
   a) he helps people.
   b) he likes people.
   c) he's modest and humble.

9. What *perseverance* that man has!
   a) He's not reasonable!
   b) He never gives up!
   c) He sees through everything!

10. Don't *abuse* the tools!
    a) Don't use them up!
    b) Don't misuse and damage them!
    c) Don't throw them away!

11. I *detest* that fellow!
    a) I refuse to test him!
    b) I just don't believe him!
    c) I think he's horrid!

12. What a *detestable* question!
    a) It shouldn't be on the test.
    b) What a difficult question!
    c) I hate that question!

13. *Intrepid* men
    a) are slow.
    b) are very courageous.
    c) cannot be trusted.

14. The teacher *indicated* the problem.
    a) pointed to
    b) explained
    c) solved

15. Don't *let on!*
    a) Don't put anything on!
    b) Don't let them do anything!
    c) Don't let them know anything!

16. Their *dislike* was obvious.
    a) They didn't look alike.
    b) They didn't like it.
    c) They weren't likely to do it.

17. She's in a good *frame of mind.*
    a) She's happy.
    b) She's clever.
    c) She's intelligent.

18. He *ridiculed* her.
    a) got rid of her
    b) made her laugh
    c) made fun of her

19. The boys are only *pretending* to fight.
a) They're only playing at it.
b) They're only dreaming of it.
c) They only say they'll fight.

20. The old man has lived a life of *suffering*
a) and swearing.
b) and sorrow.
c) and surprises.

21. I *despise* that fellow!
a) I'll never praise him.
b) I won't give him the prize.
c) I hate him and scorn him.

22. He looks *suspicious* to me;
a) I don't trust him.
b) he seems to be very nervous.
c) I think he's in pain.

23. He's a *suspicious* person;
a) he doesn't trust anyone.
b) he makes people nervous.
c) he annoys people.

24. They're *respectable* people.
a) They respect people.
b) They respect us.
c) People respect them.

25. He has a *longing for* home.
a) He's home, sick.
b) He's homesick.
c) He's sick of home.

26. She prefers to *cherish an illusion.*
a) love him deeply
b) make mistakes
c) hang on to a mistaken idea

27. Don't *bother* me.
a) Don't act like a brother.
b) Don't annoy me.
c) Don't lie to me.

28. Well, to be rather *frank*, I think he's a fool.
a) hard
b) nasty
c) honest

Are you in the *mood* to stop working? Are you *bored?* Do you have a *longing for* a little freedom from work?

Now comes the most important test of all, the test of your *perseverance!* Can you *exert yourself?* If you can — if you are strong enough to control your *impatience* and finish the chapter — you'll have a right to be *delighted* with yourself!

III. Which choice makes sense?

1. He cherishes her
   a) often because he drinks a lot.
   b) because he's fair.
   c) because he loves her.

2. He has a strong suspicion
   a) because he loves sports.
   b) because he hates to take baths.
   c) that she did it.

3. She embraced her
   a) father.
   b) attachment.
   c) tongue.

4. You need more tolerance, my friend. Don't always
   a) forgive people so quickly.
   b) look for the worst in people.
   c) believe everything you hear.

5. She earned our respect, so
   a) I accepted her.
   b) I paid her.
   c) she got my salary.

6. What presumption!
   a) He's so courageous!
   b) How quickly he sums it up!
   c) He thinks he knows everything!

7. Don't flatter me!
   a) I don't want to be flatter.
   b) I don't want a new flat.
   c) I don't want to be praised.

8. She has a lot of compassion
   a) for handsome men.
   b) for suffering people.
   c) so she didn't get lost.

9. A narrow-minded man
   a) is not tolerant.
   b) has a small brain.
   c) has a small forehead.

10. He imitated
    a) the dog.
    b) the food.
    c) the paint.

11. She petted
    a) the cat.
    b) his adventure.
    c) his admiration.

12. He's alarmed;
    a) he's under arms.
    b) the alarm clock woke him.
    c) he thinks he's in danger.

13. I know her most intimate
a) secrets.
b) husband.
c) birth.

14. He's an awful bore;
a) he needs hours to make the holes.
b) he stole the board.
c) he makes me fall asleep.

15. I was terribly bored, so
a) someone fixed the hole.
b) I took a new board.
c) I went to sleep.

16. I'm so irritable today!
a) I'm making too many mistakes!
b) Every little thing annoys me!
c) I'm annoying all my friends!

17. Her frankness is astonishing!
a) She has 12 children!
b) She's so honest and direct!
c) She loves France!

18. Is that a threat?
a) Then clear your throat!
b) I'm not scared of you!
c) Wait, I'll get the thread!

19. That meat looks disgusting!
a) It must be delicious!
b) Give me a small piece, please.
c) I wouldn't feed it to a dog!

20. The problem is, she envies
a) at home too much.
b) herself.
c) you.

21. A thoughtful man
a) is rarely forgetful.
b) is seldom lost in thought.
c) rarely acts without thinking.

22. A resolute man
a) is healthy.
b) is firm.
c) likes to solve problems.

23. That was embarrassing! In the middle of the street
a) I found a thousand dollars!
b) my trousers fell down!
c) my dog was hit by a car!

Can you feel the improvement in your English already? If not, *don't let yourself be fooled!* As long as you're *conscientious*, you'll become increasingly *sensitive to* the language!

IV. Is it true or false?

		T	F
1.	The moon moans once a month.	☐	☐
2.	Ants and bees are industrious creatures.	☐	☐
3.	Vanity is a valuable virtue.	☐	☐
4.	Faith, hope and charity are vices.	☐	☐
5.	Hatred can lead to violence.	☐	☐
6.	It is polite to revenge yourself when someone helps you.	☐	☐
7.	If you are honest with a friend, you disguise your emotions.	☐	☐
8.	Guests are people who are aghast.	☐	☐
9.	It is easy to scare a timid person.	☐	☐
10.	A person may become indignant if you insult him.	☐	☐
11.	A malicious person wants to vex other people, or make them desperate.	☐	☐
12.	A horrid little boy is usually horrified.	☐	☐
13.	All men of wisdom are wealthy.	☐	☐
14.	Arrogance often annoys people.	☐	☐
15.	A person who is greedy for money is generous with his money.	☐	☐
16.	An impatient child is likely to become restless.	☐	☐
17.	Generous men usually give grudging praise.	☐	☐
18.	Enmity is a deep hatred, and animosity a bitter hatred.	☐	☐
19.	A sociable man likes to be with people.	☐	☐
20.	The more attractive an offer is, the more eager people will be to accept it.	☐	☐

V. Find the nouns which go together.

1. injustice
2. cheerfulness
3. modesty
4. resolution
5. impudence
6. envy
7. gratitude
8. cowardice

a) joy, b) disrespect, c) fear, d) unfairness, e) jealousy, f) perseverance, g) humility, h) thankfulness

VI. Find the words which go together.

1. self-.....
2. good-.....
3. narrow-.....
4. sense of .....

a) minded, b) natured, c) duty, d) conscious

5. to cherish
6. to scare
7. to endeavour
8. to despise

e) to hate, f) to love, g) to attempt, h) to frighten

9. suspicious
10. startled
11. courageous
12. horrible

i) alarmed, j) fearless, k) distrustful, l) very bad

VII. Put in the right noun.

1. He's famous for his .....: he's never told a lie in his life.
2. You didn't get that job? What a .....!
3. He told them all our secrets! He betrayed my .....!
4. I just heard your husband died. Please accept my .....
5. Well, you're in a cheerful frame of .....!
6. She's head over ..... in love with him.
7. When he saw the enemy coming, he turned pale with .....
8. I made the mistake; no one else did it. I accept full ..... for it.

It would be a *shame* to stop now! You've already finished more than two-thirds of the chapter!

VIII. Put in the right verb.

1. Relax! Calm down! Don't ..... so excited!
2. He's violent and ..... no regard for human life.
3. Would you please ..... good enough to return it?
4. We gave him the money, and he ..... it gratefully.
5. He was angry, and ..... his revenge on her.
6. Be careful! He likes to trick people, but don't ..... yourself be fooled!
7. He doesn't care about it any more; he's ..... all interest in it.
8. He can't sleep at night; his worries ..... him awake.
9. She's always calm and cool; she never ..... her poise.
10. "I'm sure you can do it! Come on, don't ..... discouraged!"
11. Please don't ..... angry with me!
12. Behave yourself! Don't ..... so nasty!

IX. Put in the right preposition.

1. Be frank ..... me!
2. I'm much obliged ..... you.
3. Don't hold a grudge ..... them. They said they were sorry.
4. I'm annoyed ..... it.
5. You ought to be ashamed ..... yourself!
6. He's boiling ..... rage!
7. There's no limit ..... his ambition.
8. Learn to be more tolerant ..... other people.

9. I heard you wanted to see me; what's ..... your mind?
10. He took a liking ..... me right away.
11. I already promised I'll come! You know that you can count ..... me!
12. She hasn't seen him for a long time, so she's worried ..... him.
13. He was hungry and had no money. That's why she had pity ..... him.
14. Beware ..... the dog!
15. Did you say he made a million dollars? That's not to be sneezed .....!
16. He has a strong sense ..... duty.
17. I know he can do it! He's capable ..... doing that sort of thing.

X. Review: Put in the right word.

1. He has a lot of .....-confidence.
2. She's deeply ..... love ..... him.
3. Don't let ..... that we know her secret already.
4. I disapprove ..... his idea!
5. He'll betray your confidence! Don't rely ..... him!
6. Do you sleep well ..... night?
7. He never keeps his emotions to himself. He always gives vent ..... his feelings.
8. He's indifferent; he doesn't care ..... it any more.

Time to check your answers. But don't forget what we said about having *tolerance* for your mistakes!

Key

I 1c, 2b, 3a, 4a, 5b, 6a, 7a, 8c, 9b, 10c, 11c, 12c, 13b, 14c, 15a, 16c, 17a, 18b, 19a, 20a, 21b, 22b, 23b, 24c, 25b, 26b

II 1a, 2c, 3c, 4b, 5c, 6c, 7a, 8c, 9b, 10b, 11c, 12c, 13b, 14a, 15c, 16b, 17a, 18c, 19a, 20b, 21c, 22a, 23a, 24c, 25b, 26c, 27b, 28c

III 1c, 2c, 3a, 4b, 5a, 6c, 7c, 8b, 9a, 10a, 11a, 12c, 13a, 14c, 15c, 16b, 17b, 18b, 19c, 20c, 21c, 22b, 23b

IV 1F, 2T, 3F, 4F, 5T, 6F, 7F, 8F, 9T, 10T, 11T, 12F, 13F, 14T, 15F, 16T, 17F, 18T, 19T, 20T

V 1d, 2a, 3g, 4f, 5b, 6e, 7h, 8c

VI 1d, 2b, 3a, 4c, 5f, 6h, 7g, 8e, 9k, 10i, 11j, 12l

VII 1 honesty (frankness), 2 pity (shame), 3 confidence (trust), 4 condolences (sympathy), 5 mind, 6 heels, 7 fear, 8 responsibility

VIII 1 get, 2 has, 3 be, 4 accepted (took), 5 took (got, planned), 6 let, 7 lost, 8 keep, 9 loses, 10 get (become, be, feel), 11 be (get), 12 be

IX 1 with, 2 to, 3 against, 4 about ("annoyed *about* something" but "annoyed *at* someone"), 5 of, 6 with, 7 to, 8 of (towards), 9 on, 10 to, 11 on, 12 about, 13 on, 14 of, 15 at, 16 of, 17 of

X 1 self, 2 in...with, 3 on, 4 of, 5 on, 6 at, 7 to, 8 about

How many mistakes have you made?

	I to VI	VII to IX	X	
Excellent	0— 6	0— 4	0	mistakes
Good	7—12	5— 8	1	mistakes
Satisfactory	13—20	9—13	2	mistakes
Not very good	21—29	14—20	3	mistakes
Weak	over 29	over 20	over 3	mistakes

Chapter V The Soul and the Mind

Part 2: Activity, Desire, Religion

Do you *tend to* reconsider your decisions and *change your mind* whenever your task becomes difficult? Do you feel some *distress* because the last few chapters weren't as easy as you had hoped?

Well, if you're *resolved* to be an *energetic* student, if you *strive* constantly *for* command over English, and if you're always ready to laugh at your own mistakes, you'll *have no reason for worrying!*

I. What's the opposite?

1. For many centuries this city has been famous for its *pagan* temples and its
   a) free ones.
   b) heathen ones.
   c) Christian ones.

2. Do you believe some souls will be *damned* and others
   a) led into temptation?
   b) judged?
   c) saved?

3. The priest asked if we would be *redeemed* or
   a) lost.
   b) pardoned.
   c) blessed.

4. I wonder whether it's wiser to *reveal* your thoughts or
   a) hide them.
   b) be open.
   c) speak first and think later.

5. The mild, gentle bishop *authorized* statements which the Pope would have
   a) refused to write.
   b) forbidden.
   c) approved.

6. "Did your little son make that big hole in my boat *intentionally* or
   a) purposely?"
   b) accidentally?"
   c) from the outside?"

7. "When I was a child I was very *superstitious*, but my mother taught me to
   a) be more modest."
   b) trust other people."
   c) think logically."

8. Are your *spiritual* needs more important than your
   a) bodily needs?
   b) emotional needs?
   c) natural desires?

9. Is smoking *prohibited* in cinemas here, or is it
   a) forbidden?
   b) allowed?
   c) punished?

II. Which word or phrase has almost the same meaning?

1. He's *resolved* to win.
   a) He's too worn out to win.
   b) He'd like to win.
   c) He firmly intends to win.

2. "I *adore* him," she said.
   a) admire
   b) respect
   c) love

3. He has many *staunch* friends.
   a) firm
   b) generous
   c) kind

4. They *argued me into it.*
   a) They argued and I fell asleep.
   b) They finally persuaded me.
   c) They trapped me.

5. I *submit!*
   a) I agree with you.
   b) I don't care.
   c) I surrender.

6. He *declined.*
   a) He refused.
   b) He fell.
   c) He bent down quickly.

7. His *refusal* made me angry.
   a) answer of "no"
   b) statements of religious ideas
   c) second marriage

8. Which *denomination* do you belong to?
   a) professional group
   b) organized political group
   c) organized religious group

9. The *clerical* leaders tried to help the children.
   a) clerk's leaders
   b) church leaders
   c) governmental leaders

10. We met in the *chapel.*
    a) very small church
    b) bishop's house
    c) place for the organ-player

11. What does your *creed* tell you to do?
    a) conscience
    b) set of beliefs
    c) religion

12. "Living in his home is like living in *paradise*," she said.
    a) sin
    b) hell
    c) a wonderful place

III. Which choice makes sense?

1. A prophet claims to know
    a) his own will.
    b) his king's will.
    c) God's will.

2. An altar is
    a) an old religious painting.
    b) a raised, flat surface used in divine services.
    c) an older person who works for the church without pay.

3. He entered the pulpit
    a) to confess.
    b) to preach.
    c) to collect money.

4. Priests can convert
    a) Christmas.
    b) Christians.
    c) non-Christians.

5. Superstition is based on
    a) business decisions.
    b) embarrassment.
    c) emotion.

6. He's very pious; he wants to become a
    a) poet.
    b) priest.
    c) doctor.

7. I can't refuse you anything!
    a) I can't give it to you.
    b) I can't take it from you.
    c) Take what you want.

8. We concluded
    a) the letter with a request.
    b) his answer.
    c) the dog in the dog-house.

9. We concluded from
    a) the letter with a request.
    b) his answer that he was sorry.
    c) the dog in the dog-house.

IV. Is it true or false?

		T	F
1.	Priests christen babies and preach sermons.	☐	☐
2.	A prophecy may come true.	☐	☐
3.	A prayer-book is an old person who spends most of his time praying.	☐	☐
4.	A priest is in charge of a parish and all the bishops in it.	☐	☐
5.	Christians are heathens.	☐	☐
6.	A clergyman is a member of the clergy.	☐	☐
7.	All sinners repent.	☐	☐
8.	Jesus crucified the Roman soldiers.	☐	☐
9.	A prejudiced man is a just person.	☐	☐
10.	A pretentious person pretends to be better than he is.	☐	☐

V. Find the nouns which go together.

1. temple
2. clergyman
3. heathen
4. the Holy Scriptures
5. Providence

a) divine control, b) building, c) the Bible, d) non-Christian, e) priest

6. predicament
7. proposition
8. consent
9. refusal
10. argument

f) offer, g) fix, h) non-acceptance, i) quarrel, j) agreement

VI. Find the words which go together.

1. church .....
2. God .....!
3. The Last .....
4. The Lord's .....
5. the Ten .....

a) Judgement, b) forbid, c) steeple, d) Prayer, e) Commandments

6. repentant
7. energetic
8. pretentious
9. resolved
10. prejudiced

f) active, g) immodest, h) unfair, i) determined, j) sorry

VII. Put in the right noun.

1. The European religions developed from the teachings of ..... who lived in Palestine about 2000 years ago.
2. Moses received the Ten ..... on Mount Sinai.
3. The ..... is the head of the Roman Catholic Church.
4. He preached about the Father, the Son and the Holy .....
5. The church bells are usually in the church .....

VIII. Put in the right verb.

1. That's your decision, not mine, so you ..... the responsibility.
2. He doesn't care about anyone else or anything else. He's determined to ..... his own way.
3. I used to think he was an angel, but I had to ..... my mind; now I think he's a snake in the grass.
4. Relax! Everything will be fine! You ..... no reason for worrying!
5. Every Sunday, religious people ..... God in churches.
6. The first sentence of the Bible is: "In the beginning God ..... the heaven and the earth."

IX. Put in the right preposition.

1. The monk said, "Lead me not ..... temptation."
2. Do you go ..... Mass?
3. Do you believe that Lazarus rose ..... the dead?
4. Do you believe ..... God?
5. He doesn't know what he's striving .....
6. The ship is ..... distress.
7. Help me to get .... this scrape.
8. He has absolutely no reason ..... acting like that!
9. "My children never stop and think of all the sacrifices I've made ..... them," said the tired old man bitterly.

X. Review: Put in the right word.

1. Which denomination do you ..... to?
2. He's a ..... of the clergy.
3. The first two words of the ..... Prayer are "Our Father".
4. Can a prophecy ..... true?
5. Buddhism developed ..... the teaching of Buddha.
6. I wanted to say "no", but they argued me ..... it.

OK! Now you're *authorized* to look at the answer-key! We hope it doesn't *reveal* too many mistakes!

Key

I	1c, 2c, 3a, 4a, 5b, 6b, 7c, 8a, 9b
II	1c, 2c, 3a, 4b, 5c, 6a, 7a, 8c, 9b, 10a, 11b, 12c
III	1c, 2b, 3b, 4c, 5c, 6b, 7c, 8a, 9b
IV	1T, 2T, 3F, 4F, 5F, 6T, 7F, 8F, 9F, 10T
V	1b, 2e, 3d, 4c, 5a, 6g, 7f, 8j, 9h, 10i
VI	1c, 2b, 3a, 4d, 5e, 6j, 7f, 8g, 9i, 10h
VII	1 Jesus (Christ), 2 Commandments, 3 Pope, 4 Ghost, 5 steeple
VIII	1 take (accept, assume), 2 have (go), 3 change, 4 have, 5 worship (pray to), 6 created
IX	1 into, 2 to, 3 from, 4 in, 5 for, 6 in, 7 out of, 8 for, 9 for
X	1 belong, 2 member, 3 Lord's, 4 come, 5 from, 6 into

How many mistakes have you made?

	I to VI	VII to IX	X	
Excellent	0— 3	0— 2	0	mistakes
Good	4— 6	3— 4	1	mistakes
Satisfactory	7— 9	5— 7	2	mistakes
Not very good	10—13	8—10	3	mistakes
Weak	over 13	over 10	over 3	mistakes

If you look at the next page, you'll see a new chapter ready for you. Go on, you've made it this far! As we said a few pages back, *you have no reason for worrying!* Try it!

Chapter VI Social Life

Part 1: The Family, Social Relationships, Language

Will your work or your hobby ever lead you to attend an international *conference* some day? It might, it just might. Every year the number of *conferences* increases rapidly.

Try to imagine yourself at one of them. Would you take part in the *debate?* (It would almost certainly be in English.) What would happen? You'd *get the floor*, you'd *rise to speak* — but would you *communicate with* your *audience?* Would you be able to defend your *propositions* against *criticism?* Or would you *stammer* and *stutter*, unable to find the *appropriate* English words to *indicate* your views? Would you hear others *cut you short* and *rule you out of order?* Would you have to sit down and *listen in silence?*

Even if you are convinced that you will never speak at an international *conference*, we can *assure* you, without *exaggerating*, that sometime in your life you will need English.

I. What's the opposite?

1. *Daring* men run risks which
   a) courageous men avoid.
   b) cautious men avoid.
   c) dangerous men avoid.

2. That's a *trite* answer! I wanted a
   a) simple one.
   b) thoughtful one.
   c) complete one.

3. First you *flatter* me, then you
   a) starve me.
   b) pull me.
   c) insult me.

4. Don't *yell!* I can hear when you
   a) whisper!
   b) speak up!
   c) shout!

5. He *affirmed* everything his partner
   a) loosened.
   b) weakened.
   c) denied.

6. "My love, after you *rejected* my proposal I asked your sister. She
   a) accepted it."
   b) turned it down."
   c) laughed at me."

7. He's the *junior* partner;
   a) I'm the inferior one.
   b) I'm the wealthy partner.
   c) I'm the senior partner.

8. He's always so *courteous* to me, though I'm usually
   a) rude to him.
   b) polite to him.
   c) friendly to him.

9. They got a *divorce* the same day we
   a) announced our marriage.
   b) became engaged.
   c) got married.

10. Did your friend *contradict* you or
    a) agree with you?
    b) contribute?
    c) help you?

11. She's *elegant* but
    a) he's employed.
    b) he's rough.
    c) he wasn't dressed.

II. Which word or phrase has almost the same meaning?

1. He simply wants *offspring.*
   a) children
   b) a chance to get away
   c) a start in business

2. I think he's *unmarried.*
   a) He's separated from his wife.
   b) He's now divorced.
   c) He's not married.

3. He loves to be *in the limelight.*
   a) in a special light.
   b) surrounded by his friends
   c) the centre of attention

4. When did they announce their *engagement?*
   a) intention to marry
   b) marriage
   c) divorce

5. She's always talking about her *fiancé.*
   a) money
   b) circle of wealthy friends
   c) man she will marry

6. *Eminent* poets came to her home.
   a) old and wise
   b) very respected and successful
   c) wealthy

7. He's quite famous, but I don't particularly *esteem* him.
   a) approve of
   b) trust
   c) admire, honour and respect

8. We were glad to find such *hospitality!*
   a) generous welcome for guests
   b) group of hospitals
   c) host and hostess

9. That's a good *chap!*
   a) fellow
   b) hat
   c) girl

10. He wanted to *testify*.
   a) test the students
   b) pass the test
   c) speak as a witness

11. Do we live in a *civilized* society?
   a) commercial
   b) non-military
   c) educated, respected, polite

12. "No!" he *exclaimed*.
   a) wrote
   b) explained carefully
   c) said excitedly

13. He *maintained* that we were wrong.
   a) continued to say
   b) confessed
   c) refused to admit

14. The political leaders *debated* the problem.
   a) argued and discussed
   b) thought about
   c) agreed on

15. He made an *allusion* to his mother.
   a) insulted her
   b) praised her
   c) referred indirectly to her

16. She *lisps*.
   a) whispers
   b) stutters
   c) mispronounces the "s" sound

17. They couldn't *utter* a sound.
   a) make
   b) make out
   c) hear

18. He faithfully *related* their story.
   a) remembered it
   b) told it to us
   c) told it to us again

19. That's not an *appropriate* answer!
   a) proper
   b) original
   c) meaningful

20. Is the cloth *adequate?*
    a) Is it wet enough?
    b) Is it what you need?
    c) Is it in equal parts?

21. He *cut me short.*
    a) He cut me.
    b) He cut my hair.
    c) He interrupted me.

22. Do you have the *data?*
    a) dates
    b) information
    c) computers

23. What's your *proposition?*
    a) promise
    b) proposal
    c) protection

24. They called him for a *consultation.*
    a) They asked him for advice.
    b) They asked him for help.
    c) They called a doctor for him.

25. I hope you'll *back his plans.*
    a) support them
    b) delay them
    c) block them

26. His father *admonished* him.
    a) prepared him for danger
    b) warned him gently but seriously
    c) beat him as a punishment

27. They were surprised at her *exclamation.*
    a) astonished shout
    b) proclamation
    c) offer

28. We have a good *audience!*
    a) official welcome
    b) group of spectators
    c) ability to hear

29. He's a *sensible* fellow.
    a) sensitive
    b) senseless
    c) reasonable

A friend of yours may be giving a party or you may be at a *wedding* when you hear someone say, "Do you speak English?" What will you answer? Will you say, "Yes, but *please speak slowly*"? Will you *maintain* your share of the conversation? Or will you just *murmur* something and hope he won't hear you?

May we make a suggestion? Practise English now, so you can share in the social life, *discussions* and *dialogues* of the future!

III. Which choice makes sense?

1. We're related.
   a) He's my uncle.
   b) He's my friend.
   c) He's my partner.

2. She gossips too much about
   a) food.
   b) people.
   c) war.

3. The police interrogated
   a) the witness.
   b) the forms.
   c) the car.

4. She has no manners;
   a) she doesn't like men.
   b) she's too young to be married.
   c) she doesn't know how to behave.

5. "What can you give as an excuse?"
   a) "My best wishes."
   b) "Money."
   c) "The train was delayed."

6. She gently reproached him
   a) and took off her shoes.
   b) for doubting her love.
   c) so he could sleep.

7. The inspection was completed;
   a) he was full.
   b) the store was empty.
   c) he had looked into everything.

8. I had an interesting interview
   a) into his way of life.
   b) in his office.
   c) of the area.

9. I'll inherit his money because he's promised to
   a) lose it.
   b) waste it.
   c) bequeath it to me.

IV. Is it true or false?

	T	F
1. After the wedding ceremony, a married couple usually celebrates with festivities.	☐	☐
2. A festival is a public celebration.	☐	☐
3. An orphan may have a guardian appointed by a court of law.	☐	☐
4. A questionnaire is a person who gets paid for asking questions.	☐	☐

5. You have received a heritage from your ancestors. ☐ ☐
6. You describe something clearly if you hint at it. ☐ ☐
7. The most appropriate time to write out your will is in childhood. ☐ ☐
8. Newspapers are published. ☐ ☐
9. News is announced on the radio. ☐ ☐
10. A man proclaims something if he claims it first. ☐ ☐
11. Many people grumble when taxes are increased. ☐ ☐
12. A discussion can include many people. ☐ ☐
13. A dialogue is a seat in a theatre or concert hall. ☐ ☐
14. A witty fellow is one who makes clever jokes. ☐ ☐
15. People must act in compliance with the law. ☐ ☐

V. Find the nouns which go together.

1. Christian name	3. infant	5. debate
2. surname	4. lecture	

a) baby, b) speech, c) dispute, d) first name, e) last name

6. childhood	8. topic	10. announcement
7. politeness	9. conference	11. compliment

f) courtesy, g) boys and girls, h) meeting, i) praise, j) proclamation, k) theme

VI. Find the words which go together.

1. engaged	3. quit .....!	5. much .....!
2. maiden	4. quiet, ...!	6. mission .....!

a) name, b) accomplished, c) please, d) couple, e) joking, f) obliged

7. to divorce	10. to yell	13. to inspect
8. to christen	11. to interrogate	14. to menace
9. to mutter	12. to consult	15. to assure

g) to murmur, h) to threaten, i) to question, j) to scream, k) to separate, l) to take advice, m) to baptize, n) to examine, o) to promise

16. earnest	18. maternal	20. cautious
17. trite	19. paternal	

p) not original, q) father's, r) mother's, s) careful, t) serious

VII. Put in the right noun.

1. I was born on August 1st, and today's July 31st, so tomorrow's my .....
2. After my mother died, my father remarried. His second wife is my .....
3. My wife's sister is my .....
4. My wife's brother is my .....
5. My daughter's husband is my .....
6. My son's children are my .....
7. The boy's parents died last year; now he's an .....
8. He's 25 years old and not yet married; he's a .....
9. "I just heard you had a baby boy! .....!"
10. "Didn't your wife just have a baby?" "A baby? Haven't you heard? We had two! She had .....!"
11. "When will the wedding be?" she asked excitedly. "Ooooh, they'll make such a nice married .....!"
12. The bride and ..... entered the church, and when they left they were man-and-wife.
13. After the wedding, they went on a ..... to Italy for two weeks.
14. He's not a child any longer! He's 23. He's an .....!
15. Look at them! Grandmother, mother and baby. Three ....., sitting together.
16. She's the host's wife, so she's the .....
17. I have an ..... to see Mr Jones at 10:15 this morning.
18. In Italy the people speak ....., in Spain ....., and in Arabia .....
19. The ancient Romans spoke .....
20. The professor entered the room, delivered his ....., answered the students' questions, and then left.
21. I can't read a single word you wrote! Your ..... is terrible! Can't you write neatly?

Are you wondering whether you'll ever be able to speak in *meaningful, sensible* English sentences? Of course you will — if you keep on working!

VIII. Put in the right verb.

1. When our father died we ..... into mourning.
2. She decided not to marry him, so she ..... their engagement.
3. Well, I've heard so much about you. I'm happy to ..... your acquaintance at last!
4. When the singer finished, the audience ..... loudly.
5. Three weeks after the baby was born, he was ..... by a priest.

6. I ..... your pardon? Could you say that again, please?
7. Don't ..... interrupting me all the time!
8. I waved my hand, but I couldn't ..... the speaker's eye.
9. "That was your mistake! At least you could ..... for it!" "Yes, OK. I'm sorry."
10. I had to leave the room, so I ..... to be excused.

IX. Put in the right adjective, adverb or preposition.

1. Prince Charles is descended ..... Queen Victoria.
2. His wife has a boyfriend, so he's suing ..... divorce.
3. He proposed ..... her, and she accepted.
4. "Oh," she said. "I'd love to go ..... a dance with him!"
5. In England, a person comes ..... age at 18.
6. Your mother's father is your ..... grandfather; your father's father is your ..... grandfather.
7. Three cheers ..... the team!
8. I greet you ..... behalf ..... our city.
9. She spoke continuously; she didn't let us get a word ..... edgewise.
10. She turned up her nose and said, "I refuse to associate ..... such people."
11. Her father suddenly appeared, so we had to break ..... our conversation.
12. She's really successful — to say nothing ..... her brother! He's the most famous man in the country!
13. He alluded ..... the difficulties he had met.
14. He hinted ..... an extraordinary surprise which he had for us.
15. He responded quickly ..... the question.
16. I'd like to get acquainted ..... her. Can you introduce us?

X. Review: Put in the right word.

1. "I ordered you to fly over their tents and take photographs. Did you do it?" "Yes, sir! Mission .....!"
2. They ..... engaged last week, and the wedding will be in June.
3. He said nothing. He simply listened ..... silence.
4. He can't communicate ..... an audience.
5. A member of the audience interrupted me, but he was ruled out ..... order, and he had to sit down.
6. On this form, please fill in both your ..... name and your surname.
7. May I ..... a suggestion? I think I know a better answer.
8. Must people act ..... compliance ..... the law?
9. He owns 50% of the business and I own 50%. He's my .....

Now we can *congratulate* you on finishing the chapter! Here are the answers:

Key

I 1b, 2b, 3c, 4a, 5c, 6a, 7c, 8a, 9c, 10a, 11b

II 1a, 2c, 3c, 4a, 5c, 6b, 7c, 8a, 9a, 10c, 11c, 12c, 13a, 14a, 15c, 16c, 17a, 18b, 19a, 20b, 21c, 22b, 23b, 24a, 25a, 26b, 27a, 28b, 29c

III 1a, 2b, 3a, 4c, 5c, 6b, 7c, 8b, 9c

IV 1T, 2T, 3T, 4F, 5T, 6F, 7F, 8T, 9T, 10F, 11T, 12T, 13F, 14T, 15T

V 1d, 2e, 3a, 4b, 5c, 6g, 7f, 8k, 9h, 10j, 11i

VI 1d, 2a, 3e, 4c, 5f, 6b, 7k, 8m, 9g, 10j, 11i, 12l, 13n, 14h, 15o, 16t, 17p, 18r, 19q, 20s

VII 1 birthday, 2 stepmother, 3 sister-in-law, 4 brother-in-law, 5 son-in-law, 6 grandchildren, 7 orphan, 8 bachelor, 9 Congratulations, 10 twins, 11 couple, 12 groom, 13 honeymoon, 14 adult, 15 generations, 16 hostess, 17 appointment, 18 Italian ... Spanish ... Arabic, 19 Latin, 20 lecture, 21 handwriting

VIII 1 went, 2 broke (broke off), 3 make, 4 applauded (clapped, cheered), 5 christened (baptized), 6 beg, 7 keep, 8 catch, 9 apologize, 10 asked

IX 1 from, 2 for, 3 to, 4 to, 5 of, 6 maternal ... paternal, 7 for, 8 on ... of, 9 in, 10 with, 11 off, 12 of, 13 to, 14 at, 15 to, 16 with

X 1 accomplished, 2 became (got), 3 in, 4 with, 5 of, 6 Christian (first), 7 make (offer), 8 in ... with, 9 partner

How many mistakes have you made?

	I to VI	VII to IX	X
Excellent	0— 5	0— 5	0—1 mistakes
Good	6—10	6—11	2 mistakes
Satisfactory	11—16	12—17	3 mistakes
Not very good	17—23	18—24	4 mistakes
Weak	over 23	over 24	over 4 mistakes

Chapter VI Social Life

Part 2: Clothes, Jewelry, Morning and Evening Routines

We knew a girl who did nothing but learn English. So she never *dry-cleaned* her dresses, never ironed her *blouses*, and never managed to keep her *shoelaces* tied. Once we visited her at her home, and found her *exhausted*, partly *undressed*, walking over the *blankets*, *pillows*, *toothbrushes* and *pearl necklaces* which were lying over the floor of her *bedroom*. But whenever her mother told her to *make her bed*, she said, cheerfully,

> If you work until you're *ready to drop*,
> Tonight, you know, you'll *sleep like a top!*

Today she's *well-groomed*, and a successful English teacher at an American university!

I. What's the opposite?

1. Are you a *sound* sleeper or
   a) a silent one?
   b) a light one?
   c) a deep one?

2. She likes *close-fitting* clothes, not
   a) loose ones.
   b) ready-made ones.
   c) expensive ones.

3. My mother will *mend* this shirt if I
   a) get it dirty.
   b) get it wet.
   c) tear it.

4. Clothes which are now *fashionable* will soon
   a) come into fashion.
   b) be modern.
   c) go out of fashion.

5. He always looks *dishevelled!* I've never seen him
   a) well-groomed.
   b) in a good mood.
   c) looking healthy.

6. "What a *gorgeous* dress! Of course, I prefer
   a) modern things."
   b) inexpensive things."
   c) simple things."

7. Are you looking for an *artificial* fabric or a
   a) plain one?
   b) natural one?
   c) tightly-woven one?

8. This is *painstaking* work! You can't afford to
   a) think it will be painless.
   b) let it be painful.
   c) be careless.

9. I'm *exhausted* but my wife is still
   a) full of patience.
   b) full of energy.
   c) fully dressed.

10. Are you *fatigued* or
    a) fresh?
    b) thin?
    c) hungry?

11. *Relax!* Why be so
    a) lazy?
    b) tense?
    c) patient?

II. Which word or phrase has almost the same meaning?

1. She hit him with her *handbag*.
   a) glove
   b) shopping bag
   c) woman's bag for money, keys, etc.

2. She bought another *evening gown*.
   a) evening coat
   b) evening dress
   c) petticoat

3. My *bathing trunks* are wet.
   a) waterproof suitcases
   b) man's bathing suit
   c) very large towels

4. Take off your shoes and put on your *slippers*.
   a) soft houseshoes
   b) socks
   c) woman's trousers

5. Leave the dishes to *soak*.
   a) Bring them to the kitchen.
   b) Pile them up.
   c) Leave them in water for a while.

6. *Rinse* the dishes.
   a) Wash them in soap.
   b) Use water to remove the soap.
   c) Dry them.

7. She wants to *alter* her clothes again.
   a) make them longer or shorter
   b) buy new ones
   c) give away her old ones

8. She *patched* it.
   a) threw it away
   b) repaired it with pieces of cloth.
   c) used them as houseshoes

9. Her new hat *becomes* her.
   a) She wears it very often.
   b) It looks good on her.
   c) It looks just like her.

10. I'll tell you something: she's wearing a *wig*.
   a) false hair
   b) cheap coat which looks expensive
   c) worthless piece of jewelry

11. He *slept like a top!*
   a) very well
   b) like an important person
   c) very uneasily

12. I'm *ready to drop.*
   a) give up
   b) fall from exhaustion
   c) fall down the stairs

13. He was *fast asleep.*
   a) He was sleeping deeply.
   b) He was almost asleep.
   c) He fell asleep quickly.

14. *It gave him no rest.*
   a) He had nothing left.
   b) It gave him no pleasure.
   c) He worried about it.

15. I need a coat with a *hood.*
   a) attached piece to cover the head
   b) hat which matches the coat
   c) long fur collar

III. Which choice makes sense?

1. The zip broke, so
   a) my wristwatch may fall off.
   b) I can't close the buckle.
   c) I can't close my jacket.

2. I want a coat with a lining
   a) to keep my head warm.
   b) to keep me warm.
   c) because I like patterns with lines.

3. She wore a bright scarf
   a) on her finger.
   b) on her head.
   c) on her lips.

4. You stained my collar! Now I'll have to
   a) clean it.
   b) mend it.
   c) starch it.

5. I always take a nap
   a) before I go to bed.
   b) after lunch.
   c) for a walk.

6. My son's usual bedtime is
   a) 9 o'clock at night.
   b) 7 o'clock in the morning.
   c) from 9 to 7.

7. She knitted her own
   a) earrings.
   b) hairpins.
   c) jacket.

8. I spent a peaceful
   a) coin.
   b) word.
   c) night.

9. My shoes need new soles and
   a) heels.
   b) souls.
   c) holds.

10. He used the sponge to
   a) warm up his bed.
   b) cut his fingernails.
   c) wash the baby.

IV. Is it true or false?

	T	F
1. Rayon and velvet are fabrics.	☐	☐
2. Rayon and velvet are textiles.	☐	☐
3. A wardrobe is a robe for soldiers.	☐	☐
4. Many women like to adorn themselves with a piece of jewelry, such as a brooch.	☐ ☐	☐ ☐
5. In cold weather, most women wear petticoats over their skirts or dresses.	☐	☐
6. You destroy clothes if you dye them.	☐	☐
7. You can make clothes stiffer if you starch them.	☐	☐
8. A tailor-made suit is a ready-made suit.	☐	☐
9. Paper is waterproof.	☐	☐
10. You can disguise yourself if you wear a costume.	☐	☐
11. Threadbare clothes are ragged, shabby and worn.	☐	☐
12. A barefooted boy isn't wearing shoes.	☐	☐
13. You are naked when you take a hot bath in a tub.	☐	☐
14. A mattress is a sailor.	☐	☐
15. A bracelet is a small belt buckle.	☐	☐

16. Most people use a hot water-bottle for making tea. ☐ ☐
17. You can wash your face in a wash-basin. ☐ ☐
18. An electric razor needs new razor blades at least once a month. ☐ ☐
19. Women use nail scissors, nail files and nail varnish to take care of their fingernails. ☐ ☐
20. A pillow-case is a woman's suitcase, very light and made of cloth. ☐ ☐
21. Sheets, pillows and blankets are linen. ☐ ☐

V. Find the nouns which go together.

1. socks
2. pearl
3. buckle
4. shaving soap
5. wallet
6. pyjamas
7. apron
8. tub
9. fan

a) kitchen, b) sleep, c) safety razor, d) wind, e) shoes, f) bathroom, g) belt, h) money, i) necklace

VI. Find the words which go together.

1. ready-.....
2. dinner-.....
3. dry-.....
4. old-.....
5. wash-.....
6. clean-.....

a) basin, b) jacket, c) cleaning, d) made, e) shaven, f) fashioned

7. razor .....
8. beauty .....
9. nail .....
10. hair .....
11. dressing-.....

g) brush, h) treatment, i) blade, j) table, k) file

If you sometimes spend *sleepless* nights, we have the solution for you. Whenever you can't fall asleep, just get up and learn English until you're *tired out!* Then you'll *slumber* like a baby!

VII. Put in the right noun.

1. I have to buy a ..... of trousers.
2. Men carry their money in a .....
3. It's raining awfully hard, so wear your ..... and boots, and don't forget your umbrella!
4. Well, since it's time to go to bed, I'll go and put on my .....
5. Can you tell me what time it is? I left my ..... at home.
6. I knew she was married because I saw she had a gold ..... on her finger.
7. You brush your teeth with a ..... and .....

VIII. Put in the right verb.

1. "Well, I've decided. Tomorrow afternoon I'm going to come home as a blonde. I'm going to ..... my hair."
2. "Don't let the guests see the bedroom! The beds aren't even ..... yet!"
3. This morning she ..... clean sheets on all the beds.
4. Don't worry! I ..... do it blindfolded!
5. Will you have time to ..... a nap this afternoon?
6. My little brother is still too young to dress himself every morning and ..... himself every night.
7. She ..... a hair-do yesterday.
8. After he had finished digging in the garden, he washed his hands and face, ... his clothes, and drove to the theatre.

IX. Put in the right adjective, adverb or preposition.

1. She's always dressed ..... the latest fashion.
2. Wide suits went out ..... fashion 50 years ago.
3. Do you want a long-sleeved shirt or a ..... one?
4. Does he like to work ..... his shirt-sleeves, or wearing his jacket?
5. I'm going to leave her! I'm just tired ..... her complaining!
6. Her skirt falls ..... folds very nicely.
7. I'm exhausted! The children really tired me .....!

X. Review: Put in the right word.

1. My bathing trunks ..... too small.
2. "Oh madam," said the salesgirl. "Everybody's wearing it now. It's very, very ....."
3. When you sleep at night, you are under the ..... and lie with your head on a .....
4. He slept ..... a top!
5. I'm ready ..... drop!
6. It ..... him no rest.
7. "Go and ..... a hot bath this minute!"
8. He shaves with an electric .....
9. He wore a .....-made suit.
10. Do you need a hot .....-bottle?
11. Your shoe is going to fall off because your ..... is untied.
12. The room you sleep in is called the .....

OK! Now you can check your answers, study your mistakes, and *relax* a bit!

Key

I 1b, 2a, 3c, 4c, 5a, 6c, 7b, 8c, 9b, 10a, 11b

II 1c, 2b, 3b, 4a, 5c, 6b, 7a, 8b, 9b, 10a, 11a, 12b, 13a, 14c, 15a

III 1c, 2b, 3b, 4a, 5b, 6a, 7c, 8c, 9a, 10c

IV 1T, 2T, 3F, 4T, 5F, 6F, 7T, 8F, 9F, 10T, 11T, 12T, 13T, 14F, 15F, 16F, 17T, 18F, 19T, 20F, 21F

V 1e, 2i, 3g, 4c, 5h, 6b, 7a, 8f, 9d

VI 1d, 2b, 3c, 4f, 5a, 6e, 7i, 8h, 9k, 10g, 11j

VII 1 pair, 2 wallet, 3 raincoat (coat, hat), 4 pyjamas (*Am* pajamas), 5 wristwatch (watch), 6 ring, 7 toothbrush ... toothpaste

VIII 1 dye, 2 made, 3 put, 4 can (could), 5 take (have), 6 undress, 7 had, 8 changed

IX 1 in, 2 of, 3 short-sleeved, 4 in, 5 of, 6 into, 7 out

X 1 are, 2 fashionable, 3 blankets (quilt, covers, sheets) ... pillow, 4 like, 5 to, 6 gave, 7 take, 8 razor, 9 tailor (ready, hand), 10 water, 11 shoelace, 12 bedroom

How many mistakes have you made?

	I to VI	VII to IX	X	
Excellent	0— 4	0— 2	0—1	mistakes
Good	5— 8	3— 5	2	mistakes
Satisfactory	9—13	6— 8	3	mistakes
Not very good	14—19	9—11	4—5	mistakes
Weak	over 19	over 11	over 5	mistakes

Chapter VII Organizing Space, Time and Thought

What's on the *agenda* for today? Do you have a very tight *schedule* or do you have some free time to *dispose of?* If you have a few spare minutes, maybe we can *induce* you to play a game with your English words.

We're thinking of a game which needs no *planning* at all. It's called "One Man's *Distribution*" — or "One Woman's *Distribution*" — because you can play it whenever you're alone, simply by arranging words *systematically*. Just find yourself a piece of paper, then draw lines to make *columns*. At the top of each *column* write the name of a class or a group of words — any class or group you want (for example, "animals", "things which are blue", "irregular verbs", or "*temptations* and *inducements*"). Use your imagination.

Then write all the English words you know which belong in each group (for "animals" you could write words like "fox", "bear", "duck", "dog", *and so on*). You only have to be *logical:* you'll destroy the entire system if you *take the view* that a word like "bush" can be included with "animals"!

This is an excellent way to improve your speaking ability, because speaking English easily requires knowing *series* of words; you need a feeling for the *similarities* and *contrasts* within a language. (To place words *in contrast to* each other, you can title one *column* "opposites" and write pairs of words like "black — white", "top — bottom", "*destination — starting point*", *and so forth*).

Do you think this is too easy for you? OK, let's make it more difficult! Save the lists and repeat the same groups of words each week, but always try to write more words than the week before.

If you ever need an interesting way to review the words you've written (perhaps just before an examination), you can simply *put them in order:* for example, you can *subdivide* the words of one group *into* smaller groups (for example, "four-legged animals" and "two-legged animals"), or *arrange* the words *alphabetically*.

A few pages later we'll tell you about a *variation* of this game which you can play with your friends.

(to be continued)

I. What's the opposite?

1. Be *punctual!* Don't
   a) plan carelessly.
   b) come late.
   c) think only in general terms.

2. The *initial* order will be smaller than the
   a) complete order.
   b) definite order.
   c) final order.

3. It's important to decide what's a *minor* matter and what's
   a) old.
   b) important.
   c) of secondary importance.

4. I didn't hit you *deliberately!* I did it
   a) by accident.
   b) delicately.
   c) intentionally.

5. The *similarities* were more remarkable than the
   a) disappointments.
   b) disadvantages.
   c) differences.

6. Our aims are *similar*, though our methods are
   a) painful.
   b) difficult.
   c) different.

7. I always *opposed* his ideas! I never
   a) resisted them.
   b) supported them.
   c) thought about them.

8. *Uniformity* can be as beautiful as
   a) normal clothes.
   b) two.
   c) variety.

9. She has *every reason for* avoiding him: he hit her
   a) for no reason at all.
   b) for a very good reason.
   c) for many reasons.

II. Which word or phrase has almost the same meaning?

1. OK, I *won't press the point.*
   a) won't push the button
   b) won't hurt you
   c) won't insist on it

2. The whole family is *exceedingly* stupid.
   a) somewhat
   b) rather
   c) extremely

3. Do you think the police were *excessively* violent?
   a) rather
   b) extremely
   c) more than was reasonable

4. He's easily *swayed!*
   a) influenced
   b) offended
   c) shocked

5. Careful *planning* is our most important problem.
   a) building a firm base
   b) preparing for the future
   c) choosing the correct speed

6. The thieves knew how to *dispose of* the jewels.
   a) steal them
   b) divide them among themselves
   c) sell or get rid of them

7. Try to *postpone* the meeting.
   a) mail the results of it
   b) note it on the calendar
   c) put it off for a later date

8. Don't worry. The hole was *minute*, and I filled it myself.
   a) there for a short time
   b) very, very small
   c) empty

9. The women played two games *successively*.
   a) one after the other
   b) both at the same time
   c) with success

10. "I'm sorry, you'll have to take *a series of* tests."
    a) a set of
    b) a season of
    c) a serious one

11. Life is full of *variations*.
    a) basic truths
    b) frequent changes
    c) music

12. His opinion *varies*.
    a) He's usually right.
    b) He often changes his mind.
    c) His opinion is respected.

13. He thinks I won't answer a *provocation*, but he's wrong.
    a) call
    b) first call
    c) action which makes me angry

14. You're terrible! You argue *constantly!*
    a) about the same things
    b) all the time
    c) without changing your opinion

15. That's a *tempting* offer.
    a) very bad
    b) attractive
    c) limited in time

16. She's *inhuman!*
 a) She understands humans very well.
 b) She's not behaving like a human.
 c) She's dead.

17. Be *logical!*
 a) Use words!
 b) Use your hands!
 c) Use reason!

18. That *takes just as long.*
 a) needs as much material
 b) needs the same amount of time
 c) is the same number of kilometres

19. I think his letter *relates to* your complaint.
 a) refers to it
 b) replies to it
 c) repeats it

20. Their answers were *identical.*
 a) slightly different
 b) almost the same
 c) exactly alike

A few pages ago we described a game with groups of *related* words; *in this connection* we mentioned that you can play it with several people, if you *vary* the rules slightly. Here's how:

Choose a class or a group of words as described at the beginning of this chapter. Then see who can write down the most words for this group, within a time limit such as one minute. *Under no circumstances* should you go past the time limit — don't remove the pressure of time!

But don't *lay* too much *stress on* winning; whether you win or lose is a *minor matter*. The important thing is to give yourself another good *motive* for learning English words.

Now it's up to you! You have to take the *initial* step!

III. Which choice makes sense?

1. She upset
 a) all our plans.
 b) her hair into a smooth wave.
 c) in the chair.

2. He's isolated;
 a) he brought a warm coat.
 b) he lost all his money.
 c) he has no friends here.

3. He liked her; nevertheless
   a) he hit her.
   b) she liked him.
   c) he still likes her.

4. His destination was
   a) Paris.
   b) yesterday.
   c) hungry.

5. "I'm worried about the distribution. I hope
   a) we produce enough."
   b) everyone gets his fair share."
   c) the area is left clean."

6. He did well in the test, comparatively
   a) answering.
   b) speaking.
   c) thinking.

7. Variable aspects
   a) change.
   b) remain steady.
   c) are true.

8. The office of Prime Minister of Great Britain is equivalent to
   a) Parliament.
   b) his army generals.
   c) the office of the Chancellor of West Germany.

IV. Is it true or false?

		T	F
1.	An efficient businessman knows how to plan his time.	☐	☐
2.	In America, teachers grade students.	☐	☐
3.	American pupils in the fourth grade don't get grades.	☐	☐
4.	A procession is a group of people who lead a crowd.	☐	☐
5.	Newspapers have columns.	☐	☐
6.	Many Greek buildings had columns.	☐	☐
7.	A file of persons is a line of people.	☐	☐
8.	A file of papers is a set of papers which are kept together.	☐	☐
9.	In mathematics, parallel lines form a perfect circle.	☐	☐
10.	The weight of a piece of steel is proportionate to its size.	☐	☐
11.	A systematic worker is a well-organized worker.	☐	☐
12.	It is always important to see a good eye-doctor before you change your viewpoint.	☐	☐

Do you find that the time you spend learning is *out of proportion to* the results you achieve? Well, perhaps the problem is *interference* from matters which are of *secondary importance*. Or perhaps you aren't *planning your time* efficiently. Whatever the problem, *take the necessary steps* to *straighten out the matter* as soon as you can.

But don't become *excessively* concerned about your work! Don't become *isolated* from friends and family! That would be *carrying things too far!*

V. Find the nouns which go together.

1. scheme
2. contrast
3. motive
4. consequence
5. intervention
6. proportion

a) result, b) relation, c) reason, d) plan, e) difference, f) interference

7. agenda
8. reflection
9. destiny
10. conclusion
11. inducement

g) fate, h) consideration, i) end, j) meeting, k) temptation

VI. Find the words which go together.

1. three days .....
2. and so .....
3. to my .....
4. what's the ..... ?
5. under no .....
6. to draw .....

a) circumstances, b) mind, c) running, d) occasion, e) forth, f) conclusions

7. in every .....
8. to string .....
9. as far as I'm .....
10. after careful .....
11. identity .....

g) consideration, h) respect, i) card, j) concerned, k) together

12. on second .....
13. on good .....
14. on .....
15. in this .....
16. in two .....
17. in .....

l) schedule, m) thoughts, n) connection, o) terms, p) conclusion, q) minds

VII. Put in the right noun.

1. Both stamps look the same to me. I don't see any ..... at all.
2. I know he wants it very much. He told me he'll buy it at the first ..... he gets.
3. The train arrived exactly on ....., not a minute late.
4. We argued quite a bit last year, but now we're on good .....
5. I'm applying for a job. You know me well, and you have an important title; can I use your name as a ..... ?
6. Please put the bottles next to each other, so they stand side-by-.....
7. He won four ..... in a row!

VIII. Put in the right verb.

1. What conclusions can we ..... from these facts?
2. You're the man in the middle. Everything ..... on your decision.
3. Can you ..... me a good reason for the delay?
4. I have to know! Your decision will ..... a bearing on mine.
5. When will you ..... the necessary steps?
6. Young man! You're not going outside until you ..... your room in order!
7. He complained, but I went to see him and we ..... the matter out.

IX. Put in the right preposition.

1. "Good morning, gentlemen! Now, what's the order ..... the day?"
2. He attaches too much importance ..... it.
3. "It's only a small award I won. It's really nothing to speak ....."
4. The gunshots followed ..... rapid succession.
5. His speech was excellent, in contrast ..... mine.
6. America's power is comparable ..... the power of the USSR.
7. The money is only ..... secondary importance.
8. I'll tell you what other people do about it, ... way of comparison.
9. Be prepared ..... the worst!
10. In the 19th century, India was subject ..... the rule of Britain.
11. Until World War II, Britain's sphere ..... influence included much of southern Asia.
12. Her former husband had a strong character, and she's still ..... the influence of that man.
13. I just don't know. I'm ..... two minds ..... it.
14. The two roads ran parallel ..... each other.
15. Don't interfere ..... our argument! It's none of your business!
16. He learned excellent English, ... the result that his company sent him to America.
17. How can you compare Bonn ..... London?
18. He'll jump ..... the chance to sell his old car.

X. Review: Put in the right word.

1. What's the reason ..... that decision?
2. ..... no circumstances should you touch this electric wire!
3. The time I spend learning is out ..... proportion to the results I get.
4. "Don't break off your friendship with her! That's ..... things too far!"
5. "..... second thoughts, maybe I shouldn't buy it."

6. The owners subdivided the land ..... smaller units.
7. He did it ..... no reason at all!
8. What's the advantage of doing it your way? That takes just ..... long.
9. I still disagree with you, but I won't ..... the point. Let's talk about something else.
10. ..... careful consideration, we have decided to accept your resignation from the company.

It's time to check your answers, but don't *attach too much importance to* your *grade!* The important question is, how much did you learn?

Key

I 1b, 2c, 3b, 4a, 5c, 6c, 7b, 8c, 9a

II 1c, 2c, 3c, 4a, 5b, 6c, 7c, 8b, 9a, 10a, 11b, 12b, 13c, 14b, 15b, 16b, 17c, 18b, 19a, 20c

III 1a ("to upset" is irregular: upset — upset — upset), 2c, 3a, 4a, 5b, 6b, 7a, 8c

IV 1T, 2T, 3F, 4F, 5T, 6T, 7T, 8T, 9F, 10T, 11T, 12F

V 1d, 2e, 3c, 4a, 5f, 6b, 7j, 8h, 9g, 10i, 11k

VI 1c, 2e, 3b, 4d, 5a, 6f, 7h, 8k, 9j, 10g, 11i, 12m, 13o, 14l, 15n, 16q, 17p

VII 1 difference, 2 opportunity (chance), 3 schedule (time), 4 terms, 5 reference, 6 side, 7 times (games)

VIII 1 draw, 2 hinges (depends), 3 give, 4 have, 5 take, 6 put, 7 straightened

IX 1 of, 2 to, 3 of, 4 in, 5 to, 6 to, 7 of, 8 by, 9 for, 10 to, 11 of, 12 under, 13 in ... about, 14 to, 15 in, 16 with, 17 to (with), 18 at

X 1 for, 2 Under, 3 of, 4 carrying, 5 On, 6 into, 7 for, 8 as, 9 press (argue), 10 After

How many mistakes have you made?

	I to VI	VII to IX	X	
Excellent	0— 4	0— 3	0—1	mistakes
Good	5— 8	4— 6	2	mistakes
Satisfactory	9—13	7—10	3	mistakes
Not very good	14—19	11—15	4—5	mistakes
Weak	over 19	over 15	over 5	mistakes

Chapter VIII Government

Part 1: Politics, Law, Police, Administration

What was happening in the world while you were being born? The next time you're in a large library, ask to see the collections of old issues of American and English newspapers. Then look at the newspaper published on the day you were born.

What were the *inhabitants* of the world doing on that day? Were any important *decisions reached?* Did anyone *come to power*, suffer a *crushing defeat* or *win an overwhelming victory?* Did any *tyrant* declare a *state of emergency*, or *suspend* the laws so he could take away the *right to vote* from the citizens?

Who won a *decoration* and who was *convicted* of *treason?* Who received a new *privilege* and who lost an old one?

Well, to be completely honest, we have to make a *confession*. There's one little problem with our suggestion: newspapers use specialized words. For example, words like *treaty*, *perjury*, and *town council* are not part of daily speech, but they appear in almost every English-language newspaper.

And that's why we've written this chapter: to prepare you for English-language newspapers. (If you read them regularly, you know, you'll be well-informed about international affairs and feel *secure* in English.)

I. What's the opposite?

1. The ambassador *signed the treaty*, knowing that his own country would soon
   a) design it.
   b) sigh for it.
   c) violate it.

2. The prince *mounted the throne* soon after his father
   a) abdicated.
   b) took it down.
   c) put it down.

3. Most of the delegates did not know whether to *reject* the resolution or
   a) avoid discussing it.
   b) accept it.
   c) defeat it.

4. His *opponents* are my
   a) assistants.
   b) supporters.
   c) enemies.

5. The students demanded a *radical* change, refusing to accept
   a) an unfair one.
   b) a peaceful one.
   c) a slight one.

6. A political leader has both *official* duties and
   a) public ones.
   b) private ones.
   c) political ones.

7. A *treacherous* man may appear to be
   a) trustworthy.
   b) experienced and skilful.
   c) dishonest.

8. He *asserted* everything his friend
   a) forgot.
   b) missed.
   c) denied.

9. "Be careful! What you say may *incriminate* him or
   a) exonerate him."
   b) give him a fair chance."
   c) prove he's a criminal."

10. My *motion was defeated*, although the ambassador's
    a) was happy.
    b) was passed.
    c) showed no emotion.

II. Which word or phrase has almost the same meaning?

1. What can you tell me about the *inhabitants* of this area?
   a) people who live here
   b) people who own the land
   c) people who rule the area

2. He *committed perjury*.
   a) lied while under oath
   b) killed himself
   c) killed a member of the jury

3. They say he *committed a crime*.
   a) prevented an illegal act
   b) was put into jail
   c) did something against the law

4. *A secret ballot was taken.*
   a) Secret information was stolen.
   b) A man was secretly shot.
   c) People voted in secret.

5. A fool must have *negotiated* this treaty.
   a) arranged its terms
   b) refused to accept it
   c) destroyed it

6. Who *authorized* the statement?
   a) planned it
   b) wrote it
   c) allowed it to be made

7. The party needs a new *programme.*
   a) address
   b) leader
   c) statement of ideas and plans

8. They had hoped to reach a decision in the fourth *session.*
   a) official conference
   b) one of a series of meetings
   c) vote

9. The fat old king called for his *supporters.*
   a) court servants
   b) people who back him
   c) people who carry him

10. Your friend *made a confession.*
    a) made a confusing mistake
    b) spoke secretly to us
    c) admitted it

11. Don't *condemn* him!
    a) damage his reputation
    b) say he's guilty
    c) try to control him

12. Her jewels were *confiscated.*
    a) taxed
    b) taken away by the authorities
    c) shown to many people

13. He *pleaded innocent.*
    a) begged for mercy
    b) said he was not guilty
    c) said he was young and inexperienced

14. He *protested his innocence.*
    a) asserted his innocence
    b) denied his innocence
    c) proved his innocence

15. The judge *acquitted* her.
    a) declared her guilty
    b) declared her innocent
    c) allowed her to leave the courtroom

16. His *accusation* was totally false.
    a) complaint or charge
    b) statement, account or report
    c) cause or reason

17. Why wasn't he *released* from prison?
    a) taken
    b) freed
    c) kept out of

18. The police *investigated* the case.
    a) studied
    b) solved
    c) won

19. Can you *swear to* it?
    a) take an oath that it's true
    b) curse it
    c) carry it so far

20. The judge knew the *offender*.
    a) person sitting on the end
    b) person guilty of an illegal act
    c) offence

21. Don't be *unjust!*
    a) Don't disobey the law.
    b) Don't be unfair.
    c) Don't tell lies.

22. I'll bring a *law-suit* against you!
    a) legal bill
    b) well-dressed witness
    c) legal proceedings

23. After being in prison for a week, he was *discharged*.
    a) freed
    b) tortured with electricity
    c) had nothing in his stomach

24. Who is the *legitimate* heir?
    a) lawyer's
    b) rightful
    c) legally married

25. The answer is really quite *evident*.
    a) easily seen
    b) hidden
    c) everywhere

26. I want to *take legal action* against her.
    a) complain about her
    b) hire a lawyer to investigate
    c) bring the matter to a law-court

27. They took all the necessary *precautions*.
    a) borrowed the money they needed
    b) took whatever they needed
    c) took steps to reduce the risks

28. The police discovered the *conspiracy* just in time.
    a) secret plan
    b) old, forgotten law
    c) bribe

29. He died in a *cell*.
    a) room for prisoners
    b) chains for prisoners
    c) cellar

30. The sign said, "*No admission*."
    a) No confession.
    b) No admittance.
    c) No dogs allowed.

31. The cabinet *resigned* when the Prime Minister died.
   a) signed the official papers
   b) called for elections
   c) left office

32. The policeman told him firmly, "I have a *warrant* for your arrest!"
   a) reason
   b) gun
   c) paper allowing me to arrest you

33. The *penalty* is £50.
   a) fine
   b) money which was found
   c) legal weight limit

We'll teach you a sentence from the private language of the New York City criminals. (We're not going to tell you where we learned it — we refuse to *incriminate* ourselves!)

Here it is: "It's crackers to slip the rozzer a dropsey in snide."

This means, "It's stupid to give a policeman a *bribe* in false money."

III. Which choice makes sense?

1. In 1965, England abolished
   a) most of the new laws.
   b) many of the official buildings.
   c) the death penalty.

2. All nationalized companies
   a) are owned by a government.
   b) operate in only one country.
   c) are large.

3. The King gave his friend a charter
   a) to create a new town.
   b) of his time.
   c) of the Atlantic Ocean.

4. We furnished enough evidence for a conviction,
   a) so he was sent to school.
   b) so he was sent to gaol.
   c) so he was sent to work.

5. They convicted him and
   a) sent him to school.
   b) sent him to gaol.
   c) sent him to work.

6. He strongly suspects
   a) because he loves sports.
   b) because he hates to take baths.
   c) that she did it.

7. The evidence
   a) arrested him.
   b) proved him guilty.
   c) decided he was guilty.

8. The investigation
   a) registered him.
   b) showed he was guilty.
   c) suspended him.

9. His sentence
   a) was 20 years in jail.
   b) visited him in jail.
   c) was the sheriff.

10. You're fined
   a) and healthy.
   b) and I like you.
   c) £ 500.

11. A policeman's beat
   a) is usually made of hard wood.
   b) is his regular route.
   c) should be very fast.

12. His house was searched
   a) by the police.
   b) because he was a delegate.
   c) as capital punishment.

13. In America you need a license to
   a) sell wine.
   b) own a house.
   c) have common sense.

14. It was a clear violation
   a) of red light.
   b) of the law.
   c) of the Civil Service.

15. He wanted to inflict
   a) the wound.
   b) the cruel old man.
   c) pain on her.

16. The judge said, "We recognize extenuating
   a) witnesses."
   b) questions."
   c) circumstances."

17. "It's his fault,
   a) not mine."
   b) so he should get the reward."
   c) so he can use it."

18. He encourages intervention
   a) to their party.
   b) of new machines.
   c) in other countries' affairs.

19. They slandered
   a) the shop windows.
   b) the law-suit.
   c) me!

20. A city needs inspectors
   a) to clean the streets.
   b) to examine things.
   c) to prepare cases for lawyers.

21. The Queen dissolved Parliament
a) for lunch.
b) until the following day.
c) and called for new elections.

22. The judge imposed
a) all of us by his wisdom.
b) a sentence of 30 years.
c) the prisoner.

23. They suffered a crushing
a) party.
b) defeat.
c) cure.

24. He was accused of treason and was put on
a) trail.
b) trial.
c) account.

25. The decree came directly from
a) the mayor.
b) the lawyer.
c) the gun which killed him.

26. They bribed
a) the magistrate.
b) the violation.
c) the law.

The international language nowadays is English. If you want to arrange an international *conspiracy* to *overthrow a government*, you'll probably have to do it in English!

IV. Is it true or false?

		T	F
1.	In a republic, final responsibility rests with the voters.	☐	☐
2.	No voter in England has the right to vote.	☐	☐
3.	An emperor is a sovereign.	☐	☐
4.	An election campaign is the wine drunk by the winner of an election, as soon as he hears of his victory.	☐	☐
5.	The basic human rights are: freedom of speech, freedom of the press, freedom to meet peacefully, freedom to choose your own religion, and freedom to riot.	☐	☐
6.	Throughout history, most aristocratic leaders have fought for democratic institutions.	☐	☐
7.	In a free society, people who do not support the government can demonstrate at peaceful meetings.	☐	☐
8.	Some countries execute murderers.	☐	☐
9.	The authorities are allowed to summon a citizen if they suspect he has done something illegal.	☐	☐
10.	A municipality can administer justice.	☐	☐
11.	A lawyer can pronounce sentence.	☐	☐

12. In many countries, you can prove your identity with a driving-licence. ☐ ☐
13. A jury decides many cases in a law-court by following the penal code. ☐ ☐
14. You take legal action if you begin legal proceedings. ☐ ☐
15. Every community has a mayor and a town council. ☐ ☐
16. Building-licences are issued by a department of a governmental administration. ☐ ☐
17. A magistrate is a civil servant. ☐ ☐
18. You can change your fingerprints, but you cannot change your signature. ☐ ☐
19. A police station is a policeman who is standing still. ☐ ☐
20. A customs official tells you the customs duties, often after a customs inspection. ☐ ☐
21. Money circulates. ☐ ☐
22. A monarchy is a republican form of government. ☐ ☐
23. Tyrants trust democracy. ☐ ☐
24. Common law is English law which has never been written. ☐ ☐

V. Find the nouns which go together.

1. fire-brigade
2. oath
3. revolution
4. gaol
5. torture
6. bribery
7. regulation
8. status
9. ballot
10. capital punishment

a) rebellion, b) hose, c) execution, d) vote, e) perjury, f) social position, g) cell, h) rule, i) pain, j) corruption

11. plain-clothes man
12. magistrate
13. ambassador
14. sovereign
15. burglar

k) representative, l) ruler, m) robber, n) policeman, o) judge

16. suspicion
17. condemnation
18. privilege
19. reputation
20. precaution
21. legislation

p) doubt, q) advantage, r) blame, s) care, t) laws, u) name

VI. Find the words which go together.

1. Civil .....
2. civil .....
3. ballot .....
4. House of .....
5. Chancellor of the.....
6. Foreign .....

a) Commons, b) Office, c) Exchequer, d) Service, e) servant, f) box

7. municipal
8. secure
9. riotous
10. royal
11. illegal

g) safe, h) city, i) kingly, j) unlawful, k) rebellious

VII. Put in the right noun.

1. After the riots a ..... of emergency was declared.
2. A person who steals something by taking it out of your pocket is a .....
3. A person who murders someone is a .....
4. A person who is on trial, accused of a crime is a .....
5. "He attacked me with a knife! I had to kill him! I acted in self-.....!"
6. If you go from West Germany into Czechoslovakia, you need a .....
7. It's a policeman's job to enforce the .....
8. "We'll settle this problem in a law- ....., before a judge."
9. A man who enters a house secretly in order to steal something is a .....
10. When we got married, we received a ..... certificate.
11. When our daughter was born, we received a ..... certificate.
12. In 1776 the United States declared its ..... from Britain.
13. He's a successful politician and a ..... of Parliament.

VIII. Put in the right verb.

1. Of course I'll come. I want to ..... that meeting!
2. The government managed to ..... the riots, so everything was calm again within a few hours.
3. He knew what to do, so he ..... us instructions.
4. The Prime Minister wants to ..... elections next month.
5. He thought the judge's decision was wrong, so he ..... an appeal.
6. The judge asked the defendant, "Do you ..... guilty or not guilty?"
7. "Yes, I'll testify against him. I'll be glad to ..... evidence!"
8. If you want to be certain this letter arrives, be sure to ..... it when you post it.
9. Notice is hereby ..... that the factory will be closed on Tuesday.

IX. Put in the right adverb or preposition.

1. How often did the Prime Minister ask Parliament ..... a vote ..... confidence?
2. That bill would never be accepted! It would be thrown ..... in about ten minutes!

3. The new bill was passed ..... a large majority.
4. The cabinet voted to dissolve Parliament and go ..... the polls.
5. The politicians did it ..... purely political reasons.
6. Who received the majority ..... the votes?
7. The fire-brigade came late again. You know, I don't think they always keep everything ..... readiness.
8. "Keep everything ..... order!" he shouted.
9. When did you file your application ..... the job?
10. We were married ..... a justice ..... the peace.
11. The poor fellow was too old to think, so the company had to pension him .....
12. "Did you pass ..... Customs without any trouble?"
13. "I think it's legal, but I'll ask my lawyer, ... order to be ..... the safe side."
14. He was called ..... the bar, and is now a successful lawyer.
15. "No smoking! ..... order of the police."
16. The police are ..... his tracks.
17. So that swindler was finally put ..... prison! I'm glad!
18. He brought an action ..... me.
19. He's ..... the dock, accused ..... murder.
20. He was sentenced ..... three months' imprisonment, but his friend was sentenced ..... death.

X. Review: Put in the right word.

1. The Parliament in Great Britain consists of the House ..... Commons and the House ..... Lords.
2. The police ..... still investigating the case.
3. When the King died, his son mounted the .....
4. He works for the government, but he doesn't like being a civil .....
5. When he testified in court, he ..... perjury.
6. I want to take legal ..... against that man!
7. The government declared a ..... of emergency.
8. Only British citizens have the ..... to vote in British elections.
9. He was arrested because he did something .....
10. The Chancellor ..... the Exchequer was dismissed.
11. The generals came ..... power by overthrowing the old government.

To be on the safe side, look over your answers again, quickly, to see if you can find any mistakes. Then check your answers.

Key

I 1c, 2a, 3b, 4b, 5c, 6b, 7a, 8c, 9a, 10b

II 1a, 2a, 3c, 4c, 5a, 6c, 7c, 8b, 9b, 10c, 11b, 12b, 13b (c means "he pleaded *innocence*"), 14a, 15b, 16a, 17b, 18a, 19a, 20b, 21b, 22c, 23a, 24b, 25a, 26c, 27c, 28a, 29a, 30b, 31c, 32c, 33a

III 1c, 2a, 3a, 4b (*Br* gaol; *Am* jail), 5b, 6c, 7b, 8b, 9a, 10c, 11b, 12a, 13a, 14b, 15c, 16c, 17a, 18c, 19c, 20b, 21c, 22b, 23b, 24b, 25a, 26a

IV 1T, 2F, 3T, 4F, 5F, 6F, 7T, 8T, 9T, 10T, 11F, 12T, 13T, 14T, 15F, 16T, 17T, 18F, 19F, 20T, 21T, 22F, 23F, 24T

V 1b, 2e, 3a, 4g, 5i, 6j, 7h, 8f, 9d, 10c, 11n, 12o, 13k, 14l, 15m, 16p, 17r, 18q, 19u, 20s, 21t

VI 1d, 2e, 3f, 4a, 5c, 6b, 7h, 8g, 9k, 10i, 11j

VII 1 state, 2 pickpocket, 3 murderer, 4 defendant, 5 defence, 6 visa, 7 law, 8 court, 9 burglar, 10 marriage, 11 birth, 12 independence, 13 Member

VIII 1 attend (be at), 2 suppress (put down, crush, quell), 3 gave, 4 hold (have), 5 made, 6 plead, 7 give, 8 register, 9 given

IX 1 for ... of, 2 out, 3 by, 4 to, 5 for, 6 of, 7 in, 8 in, 9 for, 10 by ... of, 11 off, 12 through, 13 in ... on, 14 to, 15 By, 16 on, 17 in (into), 18 against, 19 in ... of, 20 to ... to

X 1 of ... of, 2 are (always plural!), 3 throne, 4 servant, 5 committed, 6 action, 7 state, 8 right, 9 illegal, 10 of, 11 to

How many mistakes have you made?

	I to VI	VII to IX	X
Excellent	0— 6	0— 4	0—1 mistakes
Good	7—12	5— 8	2 mistakes
Satisfactory	13—20	9—14	3—4 mistakes
Not very good	21—31	15—24	5 mistakes
Weak	over 31	over 24	over 5 mistakes

Chapter VIII Government

Part 2: The Armed Forces, War and Peace

We cannot laugh about this subject. Please do not expect jokes, games and stories as in other chapters; *bloodshed* is no joke for a normal person.

I. What's the opposite?

1. The government decided against *compulsory military service* in favour of
   a) a volunteer army.
   b) an army of drafted men.
   c) a strong military force.
2. The generals talked about *armament*, while the tax-payers talked about
   a) the air force and the navy.
   b) lower taxes.
   c) disarmament.
3. A soldier who is *heroic* in one situation may
   a) act like a man in another.
   b) defend women in another.
   c) be quite cowardly in another.
4. A skilful *retreat* is more difficult to manage than an effective
   a) treat.
   b) advance.
   c) withdrawal.
5. Our *ally* has attacked our
   a) enemy.
   b) neighbour.
   c) friend.
6. Was he *drafted* or
   a) did he draw the final design?
   b) was he normal?
   c) did he volunteer?
7. Their sergeant was shouting "*Pitch camp!*" while ours was shouting,
   a) "Put it up again!"
   b) "Strike camp!"
   c) "Defend the camp!"
8. Their ships came *within range* but then moved
   a) out of range.
   b) outside the range.
   c) in the outer ranges.
9. We *weighed anchor* 8 days after
   a) it split.
   b) we measured its length.
   c) we cast it.
10. To our surprise, the *armistice* was followed by
    a) a peace treaty.
    b) an outbreak of fighting.
    c) victory.

II. Which word or phrase has almost the same meaning?

1. The *draft* got him.
   a) artillery shells
   b) call-up
   c) barbed wire

2. Who's *on patrol?*
   a) operating the radio
   b) on guard
   c) getting the petrol

3. Who *equipped* the soldiers?
   a) entertained them
   b) arranged their quarters
   c) gave them their equipment

4. They *enlisted.*
   a) volunteered for the army
   b) put their names on lists
   c) wrote lists

5. It's an *explosive* situation.
   a) Everyone is angry.
   b) Something is exploding.
   c) Something just exploded.

6. He's *a good shot.*
   a) He's a good fellow.
   b) He drinks a lot.
   c) He can shoot accurately.

7. Who's supposed to *relieve the guard?*
   a) bring him his food
   b) take his place
   c) make sure he's there

8. He *assumed command.*
   a) thought he was in command
   b) wanted to be in command
   c) took command

9. The English leaders *allied* themselves with the French.
   a) met with
   b) discussed their plans with
   c) joined forces with

10. They rode courageously into the *volley.*
    a) stretch of land between hills
    b) shower of bullets and shells
    c) very heavily guarded camp

11. After the *raid,* everything was quiet.
    a) small, quick attack
    b) all-clear signal
    c) sirens

12. They came, ready for *combat.*
    a) marching into battle
    b) fighting
    c) dying

13. The newspapers reported heavy *casualties*.
   a) attacks or invasions
   b) dead, wounded and missing
   c) defeats

14. Our men *encircled* the town.
   a) 
   b) 
   c) 

15. That was the *decisive* battle.
   a) which we won
   b) which deceived us
   c) which decided the war

16. They *ravaged* the area.
   a) devastated
   b) retreated from
   c) successfully defended

17. Our tanks *pierced* their lines.
   a) saw
   b) attacked
   c) made holes in

18. The parachute troops *smashed* their divisions.
   a) united
   b) cut into
   c) completely destroyed

III. Which choice makes sense?

1. There's a curfew in this town, so
   a) get off the streets!
   b) I can't give you any food.
   c) you'll see a lot of soldiers here.

2. He wore the badge
   a) of a lieutenant.
   b) because he was cold.
   c) to protect his wounded eye.

3. The sergeant recruited
   a) all the equipment.
   b) 20 new soldiers.
   c) the entire campaign.

4. They drilled
   a) a hole in the wall.
   b) the string tight.
   c) the air photographs.

5. They drilled
   a) the army prison.
   b) the recruits.
   c) the ammunition.

6. Everybody joined the pursuit, until finally
   a) the man was captured.
   b) the city was captured.
   c) the area was laid waste.

7. We'll never surrender! We'd rather
   a) give up!
   b) give in!
   c) die!

8. They raided
   a) the agreement.
   b) the town.
   c) the colonel.

9. They devastated
   a) the second lieutenant.
   b) the women.
   c) the cities.

10. The generals demanded unconditional
    a) zones.
    b) range.
    c) surrender.

11. That's strictly forbidden, so
    a) you can do it.
    b) maybe you can do it.
    c) don't do it.

12. Tanks need
    a) splinters.
    b) ammunition.
    c) kit bags.

13. Firearms are
    a) weapons which set fires.
    b) rifles and pistols.
    c) political leaders who want war.

14. Air-borne troops
    a) fly in pursuit planes.
    b) are carried in air-lifts.
    c) test newly-designed planes.

15. Searchlights
    a) try to get secret information.
    b) are powerful lamps.
    c) take air photographs.

16. The trenches
    a) hid the soldiers well.
    b) flew over the airfield.
    c) were accused of treason.

17. Barracks are
    a) houses for soldiers to live in.
    b) ruined houses.
    c) emergency houses.

18. Do you think war criminals should be
    a) rewarded?
    b) punished?
    c) saluted?

In times of peace, a child playing soldier, a young man serving on a *training ship* and an old man with his memories are all safely removed from the realities of war.

IV. Is it true or false?

		T	F
1.	Battleships, submarines, cruisers, destroyers and aircraft carriers are warships.	☐	☐
2.	Pistols fire bullets.	☐	☐
3.	Artillery fires shells.	☐	☐
4.	Colonels often give orders to majors.	☐	☐
5.	First lieutenants often give orders to second lieutenants.	☐	☐
6.	Sergeants often give orders to corporals.	☐	☐
7.	A recruit is an experienced soldier.	☐	☐
8.	You can hear a siren.	☐	☐
9.	If a container is airtight, no air can get into it or out of it.	☐	☐
10.	An anti-aircraft defence system uses radar to determine when jet fighters are approaching.	☐	☐
11.	A guided missile is a type of rocket.	☐	☐
12.	A prisoner of war is a soldier in captivity.	☐	☐
13.	In a bloody battle, many are killed or wounded.	☐	☐
14.	Refugees are places where people hide.	☐	☐
15.	A cartridge is a small, strong lorry which can travel easily over fields and rough roads.	☐	☐
16.	A sentry is a messenger in the signal corps.	☐	☐
17.	Switzerland has a long tradition of neutrality.	☐	☐
18.	A conquest is a search for missing soldiers.	☐	☐
19.	In the English navy, sailors are given a naval port to drink.	☐	☐
20.	A man who betrays his country is a traitor.	☐	☐
21.	The son of a professional soldier is a garrison.	☐	☐
22.	Warfare is a system of roads built for military purposes.	☐	☐
23.	A hero is a man who is famous for his cowardice.	☐	☐
24.	A soldier is in the reserves if he re-enlists.	☐	☐
25.	A private is a person who is not in the armed forces.	☐	☐

V. Find the nouns which go together.

1. ammunition
2. sentry
3. flag
4. assault
5. aggressor
6. warrior
7. treason
8. airport

a) attack, b) cartridge, c) colours, d) guard, e) soldier, f) hangar, g) traitor, h) attacker

VI. Find the words which go together.

1. kit- . . . . .
2. jet . . . . .
3. occupation . . . . .
4. barbed . . . . .
5. atomic . . . . .

a) troops, b) weapons, c) bag, d) wire, e) fighter

6. to withdraw
7. to explode
8. to call up
9. to submerge
10. to capture
11. to set on fire

f) to draft, g) to retreat, h) to blow up, i) to dive, j) to burn, k) to take prisoner

12. warlike
13. captive
14. traitorous
15. victorious
16. defenceless

l) successful, m) treacherous, n) militaristic, o) weak, p) caught

"What a place to *plunder!*" (Marshal Gebhard Leberecht von Blücher, on seeing London in 1814.)

VII. Put in the right noun.

1. They wore steel . . . . . on their heads.
2. He was ordered to shoot the prisoners with a machine . . . . .
3. "When the bomb fell, we heard a tremendous . . . . ."
4. The USA dropped an atomic . . . . . on Hiroshima.
5. A hydrogen . . . . . has never been dropped in war.
6. The highest officer in the navy is an . . . . .
7. For religious reasons, he refuses to serve in the army; he's a conscientious . . . . .
8. The letters "POW" mean . . . . .

"War is much too serious a thing to be left to *military* men." (Charles-Maurice de Talleyrand)

VIII. Put in the right verb.

1. The enemy . . . . . down his plane and captured him.
2. The infantry . . . . . into action.
3. The enemy's positions . . . . . taken by assault.
4. The bombs . . . . . the town on fire.
5. They . . . . . up no resistance, so we quickly took them prisoner.
6. The retreating forces destroyed everything they could, and . . . . . waste a wide area.
7. India . . . . . to war against Pakistan in December, 1971.
8. Is it ever justifiable to . . . . . war on women and children?

IX. Put in the right adverb or preposition.

1. Napoleon carried the war ..... the enemy's country.
2. We were ordered to blow ..... the bridges.
3. In July 1914 Germany and France were ..... the verge ..... war, and in August 1914 they were ..... war ..... each other.
4. They issued a declaration ..... war.
5. The women and children in the battle areas fled at the outbreak ..... hostilities.
6. The notice read, "In case ..... war, report to your regiment immediately."
7. All Europe was the theatre ..... operations.
8. We learned for ourselves the horrors ..... war.
9. All her sons were killed while serving ..... the colours.
10. The US President is the commander-.....-chief of the US armed forces.
11. The advancing forces met ..... strong resistance.
12. They put ..... a terrific fight!
13. The belligerent powers entered ..... negotiations, but within a month broke them .....
14. Her son is home ..... furlough.
15. Most people have less food ..... times ..... war than ..... times ..... peace.
16. Soon after the conclusion ..... peace, many of the soldiers returned home.

X. Review: Put in the right word.

1. A rifle fires .....
2. "Watch out for the barbed .....!"
3. They set the town ..... fire.
4. Our artillery shells destroyed most of their positions, so they were forced to ..... from the area.
5. He refuses to serve ..... the army.
6. The men enlisted in the armed .....
7. My brother is a radio operator in the signal .....
8. In World War II, England was an ..... of the USA.

Key

I 1a, 2c, 3c, 4b, 5a, 6c, 7b, 8a, 9c, 10b

II 1b, 2b, 3c, 4a, 5a, 6c, 7b, 8c, 9c, 10b, 11a, 12b, 13b, 14a, 15c, 16a, 17c, 18c

III 1a, 2a, 3b, 4a, 5b, 6a, 7c, 8b, 9c, 10c, 11c, 12b, 13b, 14b, 15b, 16a, 17a, 18b

IV 1T, 2T, 3T, 4T, 5T, 6T, 7F, 8T, 9T, 10T, 11T, 12T, 13T, 14F (*note:* refuge, refugee), 15F, 16F, 17T, 18F, 19F, 20T, 21F, 22F, 23F, 24F, 25F

V 1b, 2d, 3c, 4a, 5h, 6e, 7g, 8f

VI 1c, 2e, 3a, 4d, 5b, 6g, 7h, 8f, 9i, 10k, 11j, 12n, 13p, 14m, 15l, 16o

VII 1 helmets, 2 gun, 3 explosion, 4 bomb, 5 bomb, 6 admiral, 7 objector, 8 prisoner of war

VIII 1 shot, 2 went, 3 were, 4 set, 5 put, 6 laid, 7 went, 8 wage (make)

IX 1 into, 2 up, 3 on ... of ... at ... with, 4 of, 5 of, 6 of, 7 of, 8 of, 9 with, 10 in, 11 with, 12 up, 13 into ... off, 14 on, 15 in ... of ... in ... of, 16 of

X 1 bullets, 2 wire, 3 on, 4 retreat (withdraw), 5 in, 6 forces, 7 corps, 8 ally

How many mistakes have you made?

	I to VI	VII to IX	X
Excellent	0—5	0—3	0—1 mistakes
Good	6—10	4—6	2 mistakes
Satisfactory	11—16	7—11	3 mistakes
Not very good	17—22	12—17	4 mistakes
Weak	over 22	over 17	over 4 mistakes

"I am tired and sick of war. Its glory is all moonshine ... War is hell."
(US General William T. Sherman, 1879)

Chapter IX Economic Life

Part 1: Work, Industry, Raw Materials

Have you ever thought that you might be *unemployed* some day? You never know how the world's *economy* will be in a few years.

What will happen if you have to *compete* against other *applicants* for a position? Are you *enterprising* and *inventive?* What skills can you offer an *employer?* Can you type? Can you write in *shorthand?* Can you speak English? (Your future *standard of living*, you know, may depend on your ability to speak English.)

I. What's the opposite?

1. "We need a manager who's *diligent*, not
   a) stupid."
   b) lazy."
   c) jealous of his assistants."

2. "Whatever he thinks is *imperative* is undoubtedly
   a) perfect."
   b) permitted."
   c) unimportant."

3. *Sharpen* this knife! You shouldn't have
   a) let it become dull.
   b) let it get dirty.
   c) bent it.

4. Now the problem is *unemployment;* last year it was
   a) the strikes.
   b) the lack of work.
   c) the manpower shortage.

5. "He thinks his wife is *indispensable*, but I told him
   a) she's a good housewife."
   b) she knows how to handle money."
   c) he doesn't really need her."

6. Sometimes I like to be *enterprising;* at other times I like to be
   a) alone.
   b) careless.
   c) inactive.

7. We only buy *finished products*. We don't buy
   a) raw materials.
   b) used goods.
   c) brand-new products.

II. Which word or phrase has almost the same meaning?

1. What the student really wanted was a worthwhile *vocation.*
   a) goal
   b) lifelong work for which one is especially trained or suited
   c) holiday

2. Do you want a job or a *career?*
   a) exciting, successful work
   b) lifelong occupation or profession
   c) temporary work

3. He always earned a good *income.*
   a) welcome
   b) respect
   c) money received regularly

4. His *craft* is respected.
   a) strength
   b) pair of skilful hands
   c) skilled occupation

5. He's a *crafty* fellow!
   a) strong
   b) skilled worker
   c) skilful at fooling people

6. He got it from the *workshop.*
   a) place where tools are sold
   b) place where things are made or repaired
   c) classroom

7. It's a *gilded* frame.
   a) made of gold
   b) covered by a thin sheet of gold
   c) made by a member of a crafts-man's organization

8. How can we *plane* this wood?
   a) make it smooth and flat
   b) polish it
   c) transport it by plane or ship

9. The dish is *plated.*
   a) flat
   b) shaped like a plate
   c) covered by silver or other metal

10. He *riveted* the pieces together.
    a) fastened with a metal pin
    b) welded
    c) melted

11. It was impossible to *procure* the tobacco.
    a) get
    b) store it safely
    c) remove the damage from it

12. That's an *inventive* idea!
    a) attractive idea
    b) brilliant idea
    c) new, clever idea

13. It's an important *enterprise*.
    a) company
    b) change in price
    c) major surprise

14. He thinks the most important part of a company is the *personnel*.
    a) board of directors
    b) products
    c) staff

15. The poor fellow's *unemployed*.
    a) has finished his task
    b) has nothing to do in his job
    c) is out of work

16. The child played with the *pebbles*.
    a) small glass balls used in games
    b) small, smooth stones
    c) gas or air enclosed in liquid

III. Which choice makes sense?

1. The dentist filled the vacancy
   a) with gold.
   b) by hiring a new assistant.
   c) by spending two weeks in Greece.

2. Do you have insurance
   a) that you'll get the job?
   b) against accidents and illness?
   c) when you have to speak English?

3. We have to solder
   a) our debts.
   b) the metal.
   c) the difficulties.

4. They dyed
   a) a tragic death.
   b) the wool red.
   c) the knot tightly.

5. They adjusted
   a) their watches.
   b) the thief.
   c) the accident.

6. The new shift
   a) broke off from the knife.
   b) is 40 metres deep.
   c) began at 5 p.m.

7. The British motor industry makes
   a) motors.
   b) electrical motors.
   c) cars.

8. A foundry is a place where
   a) locks and keys are sold.
   b) metal is melted and cast.
   c) lost things can be found.

9. A working-class man is a man who
   a) does manual labour.
   b) attends classes.
   c) works to pay for his education.

IV. Is it true or false?

		T	F
1.	A pay envelope is usually inside a wage-slip.	□	□
2.	Industrious people are people who work in industrial factories.	□	□
3.	All energetic workers are efficient.	□	□
4.	An apprentice who travels for his company is a journeyman.	□	□
5.	A miller is a person who owns a million dollars or pounds.	□	□
6.	An engineer is a worker who is ashamed of himself.	□	□
7.	The tip of a screwdriver is sharper than the edge of a chisel.	□	□
8.	You can use a file and a plane to make wood or metal smooth.	□	□
9.	A vice is a tool for holding things firm.	□	□
10.	Welding is stronger than soldering.	□	□
11.	Experiments can be done in a laboratory.	□	□
12.	Some cranes can lift cars.	□	□
13.	A hatchet is a hard hat for protecting a workman's head.	□	□
14.	A leather coat is very fluid.	□	□
15.	Tar is black and is used to make roads.	□	□
16.	Gravel is used to make the surface of roads.	□	□
17.	Rubber is a man who robs the company he works for.	□	□
18.	Clay can be used to make dishes.	□	□
19.	Platinum is rarer than sulphur.	□	□
20.	Copper is heavier than lead.	□	□
21.	Uranium can be used to make bombs.	□	□
22.	Granite is a small grain of sand.	□	□
23.	A glazier is a large mass of ice, usually on a mountainside.	□	□
24.	Many ancient Greek buildings were made of marble.	□	□
25.	If a manufacturer can't sell his products, he may want to order a shutdown.	□	□
26.	If collective bargaining fails, the union may order a strike or the management may order a lock-out.	□	□

If you *sharpen* your pencils and *rivet* your attention on the work, you won't be sorry!

V. Find the nouns which go together.

1. carpenter	3. optician	5. plumber
2. upholsterer	4. glazier	6. furrier

a) pipes, b) wood, c) glass, d) furs, e) glasses, f) soft chairs

7. enterprise	9. shaft	11. hairdresser
8. implement	10. mason	

g) bricklayer, h) tool, i) barber, j) coal-pit, k) business organization

12. spanner	14. vocation	16. craftsman
13. conveyor belt	15. holiday	

l) assembly line, m) occupation, n) vacation, o) artisan, p) wrench

VI. Find the words which go together.

1. a pair of	3. plaster of .....
2. blast	4. collective .....

a) furnace, b) bargaining, c) pincers, d) Paris

5. to slaughter	7. to rivet
6. to utilize	8. to procure

e) to attach, f) to kill, g) to get, h) to use

9. applicant ..... a job	10. by means	12. ..... vacation
	11. ..... return for	13. ..... of work

i) for, j) of, k) on, l) in, m) out

14. manual	16. vocational .....
15. working	17. saw .....

n) advisor, o) labour, p) mill, q) conditions

VII. Put in the right noun.

1. A ..... cuts women's hair, and a ..... cuts men's hair.
2. A ..... makes and repairs shoes.
3. A ..... makes and repairs watches.
4. A ..... prints books and newspapers.

5. A ..... sells books.
6. A ..... makes women's dresses.
7. A ..... cleans chimneys.
8. A ..... digs coal or metal from the earth.
9. An ..... invents things.
10. A ..... makes and repairs locks.
11. A ..... weaves cloth.
12. People who earn their living by typing are called .....
13. Paper is made in a ..... mill, and wood cut in a ..... mill.
14. Iron is melted and worked in the ..... works, and glass in the ..... works.
15. Coal is dug in a .....

VIII. Put in the right verb.

1. The butcher ..... the cow and cut it up.
2. Why did you buy me coffee beans? I don't have a machine to ..... them.
3. Before you put the screw in, ... a hole in the wood.
4. I have to ..... overtime today.
5. My company would like to ..... business with you.
6. Iron ..... a higher melting-point than lead.
7. He ..... a living out of painting signs.

IX. Put in the right adjective or preposition.

1. My father is not here. He's ..... work.
2. He's out ..... work and ..... the dole.
3. I'm looking ..... work; do you have a job for me?
4. In July I'll be ..... holiday.
5. Now's your chance! Strike while the iron is .....!
6. "We can't compete ..... that company! They're ten times bigger than we are."
7. It'll be tough to get that job. There are a lot of applicants ..... it.

X. Review: Put in the right word.

1. A ..... makes furniture out of wood.
2. An ..... puts soft coverings on chairs.
3. A ..... lays bricks.
4. "The pipes are leaking! Call the .....!"
5. You can write very quickly if you write in .....
6. Most of the countries of Western Europe have a high standard ..... living.

Now you can check your answers, but if you want to be *efficient*, you have to do more: you have to look at your mistakes carefully and study the words you didn't know!

Key

I 1b, 2c, 3a, 4c, 5c, 6c, 7a

II 1b, 2b, 3c, 4c, 5c, 6b, 7b, 8a, 9c, 10a, 11a, 12c, 13a, 14c, 15c, 16b

III 1b, 2b, 3b, 4b, 5a, 6c, 7c, 8b, 9a

IV 1F, 2F, 3F, 4F, 5F, 6F, 7F, 8T, 9T, 10T, 11T, 12T, 13F, 14F, 15T, 16T, 17F, 18T, 19T, 20F, 21T, 22F, 23F, 24T, 25T, 26T

V 1b, 2f, 3e, 4c, 5a, 6d, 7k, 8h, 9j, 10g, 11i, 12p, 13l, 14m, 15n, 16o

VI 1c, 2a, 3d, 4b, 5f, 6h, 7e, 8g, 9i, 10j, 11l, 12k, 13m, 14o, 15q, 16n, 17p

VII 1 hairdresser ... barber, 2 shoemaker, 3 watchmaker, 4 printer, 5 bookseller, 6 dressmaker, 7 chimney-sweep, 8 miner, 9 inventor, 10 locksmith, 11 weaver, 12 typists, 13 paper ... saw, 14 iron ... glass, 15 coal-mine (colliery, coal-pit)

VIII 1 slaughtered (killed), 2 grind, 3 bore (drill), 4 work, 5 do, 6 has, 7 earns (makes)

IX 1 at, 2 of ... on, 3 for, 4 on, 5 hot, 6 with (against), 7 for

X 1 carpenter, 2 upholsterer, 3 mason (bricklayer), 4 plumber, 5 shorthand, 6 of

How many mistakes have you made?

	I to VI	VII to IX	X
Excellent	0—4	0—3	0 mistakes
Good	5—8	4—6	1 mistakes
Satisfactory	9—14	7—10	2 mistakes
Not very good	15—21	11—15	3 mistakes
Weak	over 21	over 15	over 3 mistakes

Chapter IX Economic Life

Part 2: Buildings and Homes

Do you live in an *elegant, stately* home? Can you study in a *spacious* room with a *window facing a garden*, a comfortable *easy chair* next to your desk, a thick *carpet* on the floor and a *grand piano* in one corner? Do you have a servant who brings you tea on a silver *tray*, *lights your cigars* for you, empties your *ashtray* once an hour and quietly *draws the curtains* when night falls? Is this your life? Well, you have a number of important advantages, one of them being a chance to learn English undisturbed.

Or perhaps our description of your home does not offer a truly accurate, fair picture; your modest *dwelling* may be somewhat different. Very well, we'll try again: do you live in the *basement* of a *twenty-storey apartment house*, where salesmen are always *ringing the bell*, young children like to throw bricks at your window *panes*, a neighbour insists on playing his *piano* at three o'clock in the morning, and some old woman is always cleaning her *rugs* with an ancient *vacuum cleaner*, day and night, in the apartment directly above you? Do students from the local university visit your home so they can write sociology reports on *the housing problem? Splendid!* You have what few people have: a *magnificent* opportunity to develop your powers of concentration! You lucky person!

I. What's the opposite?

1. Generally speaking, *furnished* apartments are more expensive than
   a) unfinished apartments.
   b) apartments without furniture.
   c) simple apartments.

2. She *unlocked* the door which I had
   a) closed.
   b) shut.
   c) locked.

3. We painted the *ceiling* and polished the
   a) metal.
   b) hard wood.
   c) floor.

4. After the fire was *extinguished*, the children wanted to
   a) light it again.
   b) put more wood on it.
   c) put it out.

5. As soon as she *turned on* the light, I
   a) switched it.
   b) switched it on.
   c) switched it off.

6. She *struck a match*, but I
 a) didn't like the combination.
 b) defended it.
 c) blew it out.

7. Is the knife *blunt* or
 a) clean?
 b) shiny?
 c) sharp?

II. Which word or phrase has almost the same meaning?

1. This is an excellent *site!*
 a) view
 b) coast
 c) ground for building

2. They were the first to *erect* a building here.
 a) dig a foundation for
 b) build
 c) stand inside

3. The *pole* held up the tent.
 a) wall
 b) rope
 c) long, thin stick

4. He's managed to make his room quite *cosy*.
 a) warm and comfortable
 b) cold and unfriendly
 c) furnished in bad taste

5. We need *fuel*.
 a) a place to make a fire
 b) material for burning
 c) a hot fire

6. Oh no! Please don't *dust the furniture*.
 a) remove the dust
 b) put dust on it
 c) let dust settle on it

7. The *blueprints* are ready.
 a) blue curtains
 b) sad photographs
 c) plans for a building

8. She keeps her house so *neat!*
 a) clean and orderly
 b) attractive and friendly
 c) warm

9. We really should *tidy up* the place.
 a) polish it
 b) put things in order
 c) beat the rugs

10. I'm afraid my husband is not a very *tidy* person.
 a) charming
 b) orderly in a pleasing way
 c) strong

Do you have a feeling for the *structure* of the English language? Can you *construct* English sentences easily?

If not, you know the solution: *put on some water*, make yourself a cup of coffee, sit down at your *desk*, and keep working with these exercises!

III. Which choice makes sense?

1. Wipe your shoes
   a) tightly.
   b) with a whip.
   c) before you come in.

2. A few beams
   a) grew in the forest.
   b) supported the whole house.
   c) drew the plans for the house.

3. A few beams
   a) came down through the clouds.
   b) weren't cooked long enough.
   c) owned the company.

4. He has a stately home; he must
   a) work for the government.
   b) be rich.
   c) have a large family.

5. The bulb burned out. I'll have to
   a) water the others.
   b) re-light it with a match.
   c) put in a new one.

6. Our basement
   a) was signed 10 years ago.
   b) is made of stone.
   c) grew well this year.

7. Open the shutters, please. It's too
   a) noisy in here.
   b) noisy outside.
   c) dark in here.

8. I've never seen that sofa here.
   a) How do you turn it on?
   b) Is it comfortable?
   c) How fast can it sew?

9. His lodgings are
   a) broken.
   b) due the first of every month.
   c) not fit to be lived in.

10. I want to wax
    a) the teapot.
    b) the floor.
    c) him!

11. The glue
    a) was the strange roof.
    b) was very comfortable to sit in.
    c) stuck to my fingers.

12. The living-room windows
    a) go out on the street.
    b) face the street.
    c) look at the street.

13. A pillar
    a) can support a lot of weight.
    b) contains medicine.
    c) kills insects and flies.

IV. Is it true or false?

	T	F
1. A solid building needs a strong foundation.	☐	☐
2. A house can be constructed of concrete or timber.	☐	☐
3. It takes a long time to erect a prefabricated house.	☐	☐
4. The ground-floor is the floor below the ground.	☐	☐
5. In America, the first floor is the top floor.	☐	☐
6. A household is the land on which a house stands.	☐	☐
7. You can sit on a stool when you play a grand piano.	☐	☐
8. A tray can be used to carry plates and cups.	☐	☐
9. It is easier to dig with a broom than with a shovel.	☐	☐
10. Tea is often served in china cups.	☐	☐
11. You can hang a jug on a hook.	☐	☐
12. Wine bottles are opened with a corkscrew.	☐	☐
13. A typewriter is a person who types.	☐	☐
14. Nowadays many English people light candles with electric torches.	☐	☐
15. Americans usually keep their flashlights in match-boxes.	☐	☐
16. Sparks can start fires.	☐	☐
17. A sieve is an old building which should be repaired or destroyed.	☐	☐
18. Every apartment house has a fireplace.	☐	☐

V. Find the nouns which go together.

1. basement
2. lift
3. pane
4. sofa
5. carpet
6. mirror
7. electric torch
8. socket
9. pail
10. timber
11. nursery

a) looking-glass, b) rug, c) cellar, d) bucket, e) lumber, f) outlet, g) flashlight, h) elevator, i) glass, j) couch, k) children's room

VI. Find the words which go together.

1. to extinguish
2. to unlock
3. to tie
4. to tidy (up)
5. to wax

a) to polish, b) to put out, c) to open, d) to straighten up, e) to fasten

6. elegant
7. magnificent
8. cosy
9. tidy
10. blunt

f) splendid, g) snug, h) stately, i) dull, j) neat

VII. Put in the right noun.

1. "I don't like to sew by hand," she complained. "It's too slow. Can't we buy a ..... ?"
2. You can watch the news on .....
3. You can listen to the news on the .....
4. You can keep milk cold in a .....
5. You can grind coffee in a .....
6. You can sweep a room with a .....
7. You can iron shirts on an .....
8. You put your cigarette ash in an .....
9. Candles are made from .....
10. Jackets, trousers and dresses usually hang in a .....
11. Dishes are usually kept in a .....
12. Do you heat your rooms separately or do you have central ..... ?
13. Do you cook with an electric ..... or a gas one?
14. You can light a cigar with matches or with a .....
15. The floor doesn't look too good. We should buy a ..... to cover it.
16. He tore up the paper and threw the pieces into the .....

VIII. Put in the right verb.

1. The President arrived to ..... the foundation-stone.
2. We plan to build a large apartment house and have asked a construction firm to ..... an estimate.
3. When you come you can either knock at the door or ..... the bell.
4. It's getting rather dark. Would you ..... the curtains, please?
5. The policeman asked, "Where ..... your permanent residence?"
6. Careful! The stairs ..... steep!
7. It's a nice place, and the window ..... out on a garden.
8. This carpet needs cleaning. I'll ..... it in the garden tomorrow.
9. He .. .. the cow to the fence with a rope.

IX. Put in the right adjective, adverb or preposition.

1. The house is ..... good repair.
2. We're looking ..... a new flat; ours is too small.
3. Of course the vacuum cleaner doesn't work! First you have to put the plug ..... the socket!
4. We had a ball ..... string somewhere. Have you seen it?
5. The switch is next ..... the door.
6. He carefully leaned the ladder ..... the wall.
7. Clothes can be kept in a wardrobe or in a chest ..... drawers.
8. She lives ..... 1523 Wellington Street.
9. I locked the back door. Did you lock the ..... door?

X. Review: Put in the right word.

1. Clothes are kept in a .....
2. You can look at yourself in a .....
3. You can pick up dust with a vacuum .....
4. This town has a serious housing .....; we have to build more houses.
5. Have you put ..... some water for the tea yet?
6. We can't afford to buy our own furniture yet, so we're looking for a ..... flat.
7. Do you prefer a lamp which stands on the floor, sits on a desk, or hangs from the ..... ?
8. When the room became too dark, she turned ..... the light.
9. I ..... a match and lit her cigarette.
10. Who's going to straighten ..... the room?
11. The floor below the ground-floor is called the .....
12. I don't feel like walking up four flights of stairs. Let's take the .....
13. What happened to the window? Who broke that ..... of glass?

Have you finished? *Splendid!* Now you can check your answers!

Key

I 1b, 2c, 3c, 4a, 5c, 6c, 7c

II 1c, 2b, 3c, 4a, 5b, 6a, 7c, 8a, 9b, 10b

III 1c, 2b, 3a, 4b, 5c, 6b, 7c, 8b, 9c, 10b, 11c, 12b, 13a

IV 1T, 2T, 3F, 4F, 5F, 6F, 7T, 8T, 9F, 10T, 11T, 12T, 13F, 14F, 15F, 16T, 17F, 18F

V 1c, 2h, 3i, 4j, 5b, 6a, 7g, 8f, 9d, 10e, 11k

VI 1b, 2c, 3e, 4d, 5a, 6h, 7f, 8g, 9j, 10i

VII 1 sewing-machine, 2 television (TV), 3 radio, 4 refrigerator, 5 coffee-mill (coffee-grinder), 6 broom, 7 ironing-board, 8 ash-tray, 9 wax, 10 wardrobe, 11 cupboard, 12 heating, 13 stove, 14 lighter, 15 carpet (rug), 16 waste-paper basket (dustbin, ashcan)

VIII 1 lay, 2 submit (give us), 3 ring, 4 draw (close), 5 is, 6 are, 7 looks, 8 beat, 9 tied

IX 1 in, 2 for, 3 in, 4 of, 5 to, 6 against, 7 of, 8 at, 9 front

X 1 wardrobe (chest of drawers), 2 mirror (looking-glass), 3 cleaner, 4 problem (shortage), 5 on, 6 furnished, 7 ceiling, 8 on, 9 struck (lit), 10 up, 11 basement, 12 lift (*Am* elevator), 13 pane

How many mistakes have you made?

	I to VI	VII to IX	X	
Excellent	0—3	0—3	0—1	mistakes
Good	4—7	4—6	2	mistakes
Satisfactory	8—12	7—9	3—4	mistakes
Not very good	13—18	10—16	5—6	mistakes
Weak	over 18	over 16	over 6	mistakes

Chapter IX Economic Life

Part 3: Business

If you have unlimited *funds*, a nice, thick *cheque-book*, and no desire to work, you can close this exercise book, find yourself a sunny island, and lie on the sand.

But if you're like most of us, if you have to be concerned about *meeting your* future *liabilities*, you'll be glad to hear that *there's a great need for* English, especially in the large, international *joint-stock companies*.

There's no doubt about it: learning English is a solid *investment*.

I. What's the opposite?

1. He left the *wholesale* trade to go into the
   a) part-time trade.
   b) retail trade.
   c) parts business.

2. Prices are *going up* and our profits are
   a) rising.
   b) remaining steady.
   c) falling.

3. I didn't know this news was *confidential!* I thought it was
   a) unreliable.
   b) a secret.
   c) known by everyone.

4. My wife claims we have *ample* funds, but I keep telling her we
   a) don't have enough money.
   b) have enough money.
   c) own the house.

5. Why should I *deposit* money in the bank if you always
   a) withdraw it?
   b) save it?
   c) invest it?

6. The study showed that *consumers* buy whatever
   a) children want.
   b) producers make.
   c) competitors sell.

7. Don't try to tell me that's the *gross* weight when I know it's the
   a) total weight!
   b) smaller weight!
   c) net weight!

8. They tried to make money out of *imports* and
   a) unimportant goods.
   b) exports.
   c) ships.

II. Which word or phrase has almost the same meaning?

1. The *customer* entered the store.
   a) person who comes regularly
   b) person wanting to buy something
   c) person wanting a job

2. "Don't touch the *merchandise!*"
   a) money
   b) shop window
   c) items for sale

3. "Look! What a lovely *pattern!*"
   a) design
   b) part
   c) softness

4. Did you get the *invoice?*
   a) private message
   b) telephone call
   c) bill

5. Oh no! I've lost the *receipt!*
   a) second chance
   b) written proof that I paid
   c) instructions, especially for preparing something

6. They promised to *dispatch* the furniture next week.
   a) repair
   b) send
   c) remove the coverings

7. We're sending you the latest *catalogue.*
   a) list of articles for sale
   b) order forms
   c) set of bills

8. You've got to do something about the *turnover!*
   a) noticeable disorder in a shop
   b) amount of sales
   c) total weight of cargo loaded and unloaded

9. He hit the *counter* with his fist.
   a) person paying money
   b) person with a different opinion
   c) table in a shop for showing goods and serving customers

10. This is the *rock-bottom price.*
    a) lowest possible price
    b) only possible price
    c) firm and unchangeable price

11. The *purchasing* department is responsible for
    a) buying.
    b) selling.
    c) foreign trade.

12. We can't do anything until we see a *specimen*.
    a) group of salesmen
    b) team of special experts
    c) sample

III. Which choice makes sense?

1. We shall execute
    a) the chickens immediately.
    b) our losses immediately.
    c) your order immediately.

2. If you can't meet your liabilities,
    a) telephone them.
    b) borrow some money.
    c) order more merchandise.

3. Secretly, he dealt in securities, especially
    a) automobile insurance.
    b) office safes.
    c) stocks.

4. This is rather a slack period. Business is
    a) not too good.
    b) normal.
    c) excellent.

5. We invested in
    a) the price.
    b) the loss.
    c) the company.

6. Enclosed is
    a) the thief as well as his wife.
    b) a check for $10.
    c) the factory.

7. How many items
    a) are on your list?
    b) are in your bank account?
    c) did the price go up?

8. A joint-stock company is owned by
    a) the joints.
    b) the stocks.
    c) the owners of the stocks.

9. "What can you offer as security for this loan?"
    a) "My wife."
    b) "My house."
    c) "Immediate payment."

10. He works at the stock exchange,
    a) selling to warehouses.
    b) selling securities.
    c) exchanging articles.

You won't need a foreign language if you shop only at your local *grocer's* or *butcher's*, but what language will you speak if you visit a *supermarket* or a *department store* in a foreign country?

IV. Is it true or false?

		T	F
1.	Most businessmen try to help their competitors.	☐	☐
2.	If merchandise gets damaged before it is sold, it has a trade-mark.	☐	☐
3.	A cargo is a new car which is ready to be driven.	☐	☐
4.	A cheque-book is a small book of cheques.	☐	☐
5.	A store has a clearance sale if it sells cleaning materials, such as soap.	☐	☐
6.	A warehouse is a department store.	☐	☐
7.	Publicity is a service provided by a city for the public, such as public buses.	☐	☐
8.	An enclosure is something included with a letter in an envelope.	☐	☐
9.	A businessman may pay his debts with a bill of exchange.	☐	☐
10.	A surplus is a man who has many children.	☐	☐

V. Find the nouns which go together.

1. purchaser
2. proprietor
3. invoice
4. consumer
5. consumption
6. currency

a) receipt, b) buyer, c) money, d) user, e) use, f) owner

7. butcher's
8. baker's
9. grocer's
10. department store
11. bank

g) clothes, h) food, i) meat, j) cheque-book, k) bread

VI. Find the words which go together.

1. gratis
2. surplus
3. confidential
4. ample
5. secure

a) secret, b) extra, c) free of charge, d) safe, e) enough

6. to make .....
7. to go .....
8. to settle an .....
9. to fetch a good .....
10. to pay by .....

f) price, g) bankrupt, h) account, i) inquiries, j) cheque

VII. Put in the right noun.

1. Do I have to pay in cash? Won't you accept a .....?
2. I only have a ten-pound ..... in my pocket.
3. I only have a ten-dollar ..... in my pocket.

4. What's the ..... of exchange between the dollar and the German mark?
5. I put my money in a savings-bank, and earned a good rate of .....
6. Many businessmen are members of the Chamber of .....
7. Someone who owes money is a .....

VIII. Put in the right verb.

1. "May I ..... you?" the shop assistant asked.
2. "I'd like to ..... a look at those shoes," she answered.
3. "What size shoe do you .....?"
4. "Do you ..... any special preferences?"
5. She looked at several dresses, and then ..... her choice.
6. "The demand is too great and our supplies are too limited. We just can't ..... the demand."
7. I'll ..... the money from my bank account to yours.
8. He had a small business, but it ..... bankrupt.

What will you do if you work for a large international company? *Transfer* money internationally? Plan *investments* in foreign countries? *Make inquiries* in another country, or *execute* orders from foreign customers? Be responsible for the safe arrival of *cargoes* in foreign ports, or for foreign *deliveries?*

IX. Put in the right adverb or preposition.

1. I've got good merchandise but I can't find an outlet ..... it!
2. He sells corn; in fact, I think he deals ..... all kinds of grain.
3. Sales are terrible! Our business has really fallen .....!
4. We sincerely regret the need to inform you of a delay ..... payment.
5. I'm happy to announce that there's an increased demand .... our products.
6. Can you give me change ..... a ten-pound note?
7. He wants to withdraw money ..... the bank.
8. Man! Did I spend a lot ..... money today!
9. We can sell it ..... a good price.
10. The shop assistant asked, "What can I do ..... you?"
11. She tried ..... almost all the shoes in the shop.
12. "Shall I wrap them ..... for you?"
13. "He and I agreed to charge the same prices. We just don't want to compete ..... each other."
14. We are sending the delivery ..... approval. If you are not satisfied, you can return the merchandise and pay nothing.
15. We reckoned ..... the bill.

X. Review: Put in the right word.

1. I deposited the money in a savings- . . . . .
2. He's in the retail . . . . .
3. You can buy clothes, furniture, toys, etc. in a . . . . . store.
4. I have very little money with me. May I give you a cheque or must I pay in . . . . . ?
5. You can buy bread at a . . . . .
6. You can buy meat at a . . . . .
7. I'm not so sure about that company. I think we ought to . . . . . inquiries before we give them credit.
8. Can I pay . . . . . cheque ?
9. "We'll give you this sample free . . . . . charge."

Key

I 1b, 2c, 3c, 4a, 5a, 6b, 7c, 8b

II 1b, 2c, 3a, 4c, 5b, 6b (*alternative spelling:* despatch), 7a, 8b, 9c, 10a, 11a, 12c

III 1c, 2b, 3c, 4a, 5c, 6b, 7a, 8c, 9b, 10b

IV 1F, 2F, 3F, 4T, 5F, 6F, 7F, 8T, 9T, 10F

V 1b, 2f, 3a, 4d, 5e, 6c, 7i, 8k, 9h, 10g, 11j

VI 1c, 2b, 3a, 4e, 5d, 6i, 7g, 8h, 9f, 10j

VII 1 cheque (*Am* check), 2 note, 3 bill, 4 rate, 5 interest, 6 Commerce, 7 debtor

VIII 1 help, 2 have, 3 take, 4 have, 5 made, 6 meet (keep up with), 7 transfer, 8 went

IX 1 for, 2 in, 3 off, 4 in, 5 for, 6 for, 7 from, 8 of, 9 at, 10 for, 11 on, 12 up, 13 with (against), 14 on, 15 up

X 1 bank (account), 2 trade, 3 department, 4 cash, 5 baker's, 6 butcher's, 7 make, 8 by, 9 of

How many mistakes have you made?

	I to VI	VII to IX	X
Excellent	0— 3	0— 3	0—1 mistakes
Good	4— 6	4— 6	2 mistakes
Satisfactory	7—10	7—10	3 mistakes
Not very good	11—15	11—15	4 mistakes
Weak	over 15	over 15	over 4 mistakes

Chapter IX Economic Life

Part 4: Restaurant, Café, Hotel

Now you're in trouble! You're about to begin the chapter on food, a chapter filled with sentences about *exquisite* meals. What will happen? Will you begin to imagine plates of *juicy, delicious roast meat* covered with rich *gravy*, placed next to *mashed potatoes* and a *tasty salad*, accompanied by a fine wine and followed by cake or *chocolate* ice-cream? Will your mouth begin to water, and your stomach begin to complain? Will you stop working so you can *eat your fill?* And what will happen then? Will you be too *sleepy* to continue work?

Don't say we didn't warn you! Our advice is, use your will-power! Even if interesting sounds and attractive smells start coming to you from the kitchen, forget them! Don't listen if you hear someone *preparing a meal, frying* meat, *peeling* apples and *toasting* bread. If you put down your pen to walk towards the food, you won't get back to work for hours! Wait until you hear the call "*Dinner is ready* — come and *set the table*, please!" Then you'll be able to enjoy a *substantial* meal with a clear conscience.

On the other hand, if you don't like to *work on an empty stomach*, or if you feel you're *starving to death*, we wouldn't suggest you sit quietly and suffer. Just *spread some butter on a slice of bread*, make yourself something to drink and come back to our book *refreshed*.

I. What's the opposite?

1. You promised me a *juicy* piece of meat and gave me a
   a) dry piece.
   b) tender piece.
   c) lean piece.

2. My doctor thinks I'm a *heavy drinker*. What a fool he is! I
   a) only like light drinks.
   b) didn't gain weight by drinking.
   c) never drink anything alcoholic.

3. We serve both *alcoholic beverages* and
   a) light drinks.
   b) soft drinks.
   c) easy drinks.

4. Less than an hour after he *quenched his thirst* he
   a) drank something.
   b) became thirsty.
   c) started complaining about it.

5. Everything you cook is *delicious;* everything I cook is
   a) tasteless.
   b) light.
   c) heavy.

6. "*Are you full?*" "No,
   a) I'm still sleepy."
   b) I'm still thirsty."
   c) I'm still hungry."

II. Which word or phrase has almost the same meaning?

1. He loves nothing more than a *feast!*
   a) holiday
   b) large, excellent meal
   c) dance

2. They sat down to a long *banquet.*
   a) low table
   b) bench attached to a table
   c) large meal for a special event

3. Somebody told me there's a *luxurious* hotel in this town.
   a) very large
   b) expensive and very comfortable
   c) famous

4. Could you *clear the table,* please?
   a) take everything off it
   b) wipe it
   c) make it shiny

5. She loves *fried* potatoes.
   a) boiled
   b) baked
   c) cooked in oil

6. I hope the cook *tasted* this soup.
   a) added tasty spices
   b) tested it on a guest
   c) ate a little to check if it was good

7. I met her in a *cafeteria.*
   a) self-service restaurant
   b) small restaurant mainly for coffee
   c) place with self-service coffee machines

8. Your cooking is truly *exquisite!*
   a) very expensive
   b) delicate and delicious
   c) carefully prepared

9. That was a good *chop!*
   a) hotel guard
   b) red wine
   c) piece of meat with bone in it

III. Which choice makes sense?

1. The cow chewed
   a) the milk.
   b) the grass.
   c) her own tail.

2. I like my toast
   a) red and juicy.
   b) boiled well.
   c) golden brown.

3. Spread the red tablecloth
   a) on the plate.
   b) on the table.
   c) around the cow's neck.

4. It tasted as sour as
   a) a rotting fish.
   b) a lemon.
   c) sugar.

5. It tasted as sweet as
   a) roast meat.
   b) an unripe apple.
   c) honey.

6. She peeled the
   a) potatoes.
   b) bones.
   c) jam on the bread.

7. Mashed potatoes
   a) grow in the earth.
   b) should be creamy.
   c) are fried in oil.

8. She squeezed the
   a) orange.
   b) ale.
   c) raw egg.

9. What a rotten pear!
   a) Cook it.
   b) Eat it.
   c) Throw it away.

10. He seasoned
    a) the bottle tightly.
    b) at the hotel.
    c) the meat.

11. If you want to make a sandwich, you'll need
    a) sand.
    b) several shovels.
    c) bread.

12. Would you like strawberries and cream for
    a) desert?
    b) dessert?
    c) pastry?

IV. Is it true or false?

		T	F
1.	Gravy is made from meat juices.	☐	☐
2.	You can buy ale in a pub.	☐	☐
3.	A boarding-house is a place for training hotel staff.	☐	☐
4.	In winter, some people put a hot sauce in their beds at night to warm them.	☐	☐
5.	You can put lettuce, cucumber, tomatoes, onions and radishes into a salad.	☐	☐
6.	A herring is a round fruit, yellow or orange, and smaller than a peach.	☐	☐
7.	Poultry is the party held the evening before a wedding.	☐	☐
8.	You make scrambled eggs by boiling eggs in water for 3 to 5 minutes.	☐	☐
9.	You make fried eggs by cooking them without their shells in boiling water.	☐	☐
10.	Plums and cabbages are fruits.	☐	☐
11.	Gooseberries are a kind of grain which is fed to geese, ducks and chickens, especially in the United States.	☐	☐
12.	Raspberries are red.	☐	☐
13.	Spinach is green.	☐	☐
14.	Wine is made from grapes.	☐	☐
15.	Many wine bottles are closed with corks.	☐	☐
16.	A sausage is a female pig.	☐	☐
17.	Brandy, whisky and punch are alcoholic drinks.	☐	☐

V. Find the nouns which go together.

1. feast
2. poultry
3. preserves
4. herring
5. ale
6. spirits
7. spice
8. bill

a) beer, b) check, c) fish, d) chicken, e) banquet, f) jam, g) pepper, h) alcohol

VI. Find the words which go together.

1. to feast
2. to squeeze
3. to fry
4. to flavour
5. to starve
6. to relax

a) to be hungry, b) to cook, c) to eat well, d) to rest, e) to press, f) to season

7. scanty
8. substantial
9. sleepy
10. sleepless
11. tasty

g) tired, h) solid, i) awake, j) meagre, k) well-flavoured

VII. Put in the right noun.

1. The meat from a sheep is called .....
2. The meat from a calf is called .....
3. The meat from a pig is called .....
4. "No, thank you. I never drink alcoholic ....."
5. What would you like for .....: ice-cream or cake?
6. After having finished the meal he said, "Waiter, the ..... please."
7. Would you like to drink some orange-.....?
8. I hope I haven't put too much lemon-..... in the tomato salad.
9. How much whipped ..... do you want on your cake?
10. When our children travelled through Europe on bicycles, they slept in ..... hostels.

VIII. Put in the right verb.

1. We ..... the night in a small hotel.
2. He ..... an upset stomach.
3. I couldn't get to sleep! I ..... awake all night.
4. I haven't eaten since yesterday! I'm ..... to death!
5. Many people like to rest after a large meal, to give their stomachs a chance to ..... the food.
6. My uncle likes to ..... drunk once a week.
7. That pear is so old; it must have ..... by now.

IX. Put in the missing adjective or preposition.

1. Is everything included ..... the price?
2. It tastes ..... vinegar.
3. Do you like your meat rare, medium or .....?
4. This restaurant is famous for its roast beef, but I really don't have an appetite ..... beef tonight.
5. Shall I spread some butter ..... this bread for you?
6. We drank ..... the health of the Queen of England.

X. Review: Put in the right word.

1. Can you work well ..... an empty stomach?
2. A ..... serves you in a restaurant.
3. Could you cut me a ..... of bread, please?
4. ..... you full?
5. You can mix lettuce, cucumber and tomatoes to make a tasty .....
6. Dinner is ready. I just have to ..... the table and then we can eat.
7. Shall I pour some ..... over your meat and your mashed potatoes?

Key

I 1a, 2c, 3b, 4b, 5a, 6c

II 1b, 2c, 3b, 4a, 5c, 6c, 7a, 8b, 9c

III 1b, 2c, 3b, 4b, 5c, 6a, 7b, 8a, 9c, 10c, 11c, 12b

IV 1T, 2T, 3F, 4F, 5T, 6F, 7F, 8F, 9F, 10F, 11F, 12T, 13T, 14T, 15T, 16F, 17T

V 1e, 2d, 3f, 4c, 5a, 6h, 7g, 8b

VI 1c, 2e, 3b, 4f, 5a, 6d, 7j, 8h, 9g, 10i, 11k

VII 1 mutton, 2 veal, 3 pork, 4 beverages (drinks), 5 dessert, 6 bill (*Am* check), 7 juice (squash), 8 juice, 9 cream, 10 youth

VIII 1 spent (stayed), 2 has (had), 3 lay (stayed, was), 4 starving, 5 digest, 6 get, 7 rotted

IX 1 in, 2 of (like), 3 well done, 4 for, 5 on, 6 to

X 1 on, 2 waiter (waitress), 3 slice, 4 Are, 5 salad, 6 lay (set), 7 gravy

How many mistakes have you made?

	I to VI	VII to IX	X
Excellent	0— 3	0— 2	0 mistakes
Good	4— 6	3— 4	1 mistakes
Satisfactory	7—10	5— 7	2 mistakes
Not very good	11—16	8—11	3 mistakes
Weak	over 16	over 11	over 3 mistakes

Chapter IX Economic Life

Part 5: Agriculture, Riches and Poverty

A neighbour of ours has a son studying at the school for *agriculture*. When he came home for a vacation we began chatting with him, and happened to ask if he needed English in his studies.

"Well," he said, "I'm reading a book now which comes from America, on the *cultivation* of *barley*. And I'm supposed to be reading a book on *cattle-breeding*, which was published in Texas or California or somewhere like that. Our book on *greenhouses* was in English — also a book on *flower-beds*. Lots of *fertilizers* come from America and Canada, so we read about them in English sometimes. *Combines*, too. Funny, isn't it? I learned English only when I really had to. At first it was tough, but I just *took the bull by the horns* and studied it."

I. What's the opposite?

1. He *prospered* while his assistant
   a) became poorer.
   b) didn't work at all.
   c) stayed in the office.

2. Our son lives in *abundance* while we live
   a) in a farming area.
   b) in poverty.
   c) in an old house.

3. The newspapers wrote that he *is rolling in money*, but I know he
   a) doesn't waste any money.
   b) has no money.
   c) lives very simply.

4. With modern science, man is able to turn *barren* land into
   a) a valley.
   b) fertile land.
   c) a man-made lake.

5. That bull seems *fierce*, but he's really
   a) quite sick.
   b) not particularly valuable.
   c) very gentle.

6. He likes *savage* dogs and
   a) tame women.
   b) foolish women.
   c) young, exciting women.

7. Before you came the garden was *neglected;* now
   a) it's ruined.
   b) it's well-cared for.
   c) the fence is gone.

8. Southern England is *fertile;* the north of Scotland is
   a) cold.
   b) wild.
   c) poor for agriculture.

The farmer took the stranger to the *pig-sty*, to show him the pigs. "They look strong and healthy," said the stranger, politely.

"Strong and healthy! Stranger, I tell you, one of my pigs once swallowed ten cases of dynamite before I could stop him. Then the *bull* came along and knocked him over the fence. The *pig-sty* was destroyed, all the windows in the *farmhouse* were smashed, and we found parts of that bull half a mile away."

"What happened to the pig?"

"Well, I'll tell you, stranger. For a few weeks we had a really sick pig."

II. Which word or phrase has almost the same meaning?

1. He struggled to *augment* his income.
   a) recover
   b) keep
   c) increase
2. We need a new *combine.*
   a) combination of crops
   b) mixture of types of fertilizer
   c) machine for harvesting grain
3. It won't be easy to *drain* this land!
   a) clear it
   b) remove the water from it
   c) cultivate it
4. He's an expert in *cattle-breeding*
   a) raising cattle
   b) roping cattle
   c) stealing cattle
5. The horses have to be *watered.*
   a) washed
   b) given water to drink
   c) taken to the river
6. The bird sat on the *hedge.*
   a) row of bushes or low trees
   b) dead tree lying on the ground
   c) wooden fence
7. The boy shot the *fowl.*
   a) He made a mistake.
   b) He shot the chickens.
   c) He shot the wild dogs.

8. They were *well-to-do.*
   a) were always ready to help
   b) were healthy and active
   c) had enough money to live well

9. She's in great *distress.*
   a) without clothes
   b) under pressure of time
   c) in pain or sorrow

10. He ran into the *shed.*
   a) area without sunlight
   b) small building for tools, etc.
   c) pile of fertilizer

III. Which choice makes sense?

1. The women plucked
   a) the chickens.
   b) the cows.
   c) into the river.

2. Take the rake and
   a) water the garden.
   b) feed it to the geese.
   c) gather up the dead leaves.

3. Rabbits are
   a) smaller than mice.
   b) about as large as mice.
   c) larger than mice.

4. An orchard is
   a) a place to breed chickens.
   b) a garden of fruit trees.
   c) the cow who leads the herd.

5. Take the spade and
   a) brush the horses.
   b) turn the cream into butter.
   c) dig in the garden.

6. He has a large estate
   a) of servants.
   b) in the country.
   c) in his trousers.

7. A mature man
   a) has a school degree.
   b) is experienced and thoughtful.
   c) is a skilful farmer.

8. A prosperous man
   a) is well-to-do.
   b) works hard.
   c) is seldom home.

9. He expected a full pension
   a) but they only served breakfast.
   b) because he broke his leg.
   c) after 30 years in the factory.

10. This hose
a) is where the pigs are kept.
b) was worn by my grandfather.
c) was bought in a gardening shop.

A slow train stopped in a *rural* area, far from any station. A passenger asked one of the railroad workers, "Why have we stopped?"

"There's a *herd* of cows on the tracks," was the answer.

The train finally began to move forward, but half an hour later it stopped again. The passenger, completely out of patience, asked, "What's the matter now?"

"We've caught up with that *herd* of cows again."

IV. Is it true or false?

	T	F
1. Farmers reap corn when it has ripened.	☐	☐
2. A stable is a well-built farmhouse.	☐	☐
3. In America, cows are kept in a barn.	☐	☐
4. A dog-kennel is a dish for the dog's food.	☐	☐
5. A cow is female and a bull is male.	☐	☐
6. Many people have dogs or cats as pets.	☐	☐
7. If you want to get into a locked house, you need a turkey to open the door.	☐	☐
8. A pig-sty is a farmer who breeds pigs.	☐	☐
9. Rats are larger than beetles.	☐	☐
10. Horses have paws and cats have hoofs.	☐	☐
11. Most horseshoes are made of wood.	☐	☐
12. Snakes hiss.	☐	☐
13. Unhappy dogs whine.	☐	☐
14. Apple-trees, cherry-trees, pear-trees and plum-trees all bear fruit.	☐	☐
15. Birch trees have white bark.	☐	☐
16. Chestnut trees bear chestnuts.	☐	☐
17. Beech trees only grow near the seaside.	☐	☐
18. Fir trees have pointed leaves that look like needles.	☐	☐
19. Lilacs are either white or orange.	☐	☐
20. Horses and cows eat hay and clover.	☐	☐
21. Barley, rye and oats are farm animals.	☐	☐
22. A pasture is a method for making milk safe to drink.	☐	☐

"He forgot to turn off his electric milking-machine."
"What happened?"
"The next time he went to the *barn* he found his cow turned inside out."

V. Find the nouns which go together.

1. agriculture
2. lawn
3. foliage
4. bough
5. shrub
6. hothouse
7. bouquet
8. lane
9. dove

a) greenhouse, b) flowers, c) leaves, d) pigeon, e) branch, f) farming, g) grass, h) bush, i) path

VI. Find the words which go together.

1. to augment
2. to drain
3. to ripen
4. to pet
5. to breed
6. to pluck

a) to pat, b) to become mature, c) to pick, d) to increase, e) to remove the water, f) to raise animals

7. to feed .....
8. to thresh .....
9. to glide .....
10. to graze .....
11. to crawl .....

g) in the air, h) corn, i) the chickens, j) on all fours, k) in the pasture

The 14-year-old daughter, listening to her favourite music on the radio — very loud — asked her father, "Have you ever heard anything so wonderful?"

"Well," said the father, "I once heard a crash between a lorry carrying milk-bottles and a car filled with excited *turkeys*."

VII. Put in the right noun.

1 A man who owns land is a .....
2. A farmer keeps hay in a .....
3. Barking ..... seldom bite.
4. A man who takes care of sheep is a .....
5. A man who takes care of a garden is a .....
6. Grapes grow on .....
7. You can buy a bouquet of flowers in a .....
8. A large farm which produces tobacco, tea or cotton is a .....

A boy from the city, visiting his *rural* relatives for the first time, watched one evening as his aunt *plucked* a chicken. After a few minutes the boy asked, "Aunt Julia, do you have to take their clothes off every night?"

VIII. Put in the right verb.

1. We spend as much as we earn; we just manage to ..... both ends meet.
2. Beggars ..... be choosers.
3. When the old woman died, she ..... a considerable fortune to her grandchildren.
4. It's her birthday. I want to ..... her a present.
5. Don't worry. My dog doesn't .....
6. The grass is getting too high. I suppose it's time to ..... the lawn again.
7. Roses ..... lovely.
8. ..... hay while the sun shines.

IX. Put in the right preposition.

1. He's unbelievably rich! He's just rolling ..... money!
2. They never know if they'll have enough money for the next meal. They live ..... hand ..... mouth.
3. Over half the people in the world live ..... utter misery.
4. We've been happy ever since we moved ..... the country.
5. He owns a large herd ..... cattle.
6. His brother owns 20 head ..... cattle.
7. I have an awful lot to do, but ..... a pinch I could drive you to the station.
8. These roses are well-cared .....!
9. Let's buy a bunch ..... flowers.

X. Review: Put in the right word.

1. Young children like to crawl ..... all fours.
2. Flowers grow in flower-.....
3. Take the bull ..... the horns!
4. The cows are grazing ..... the pasture.
5. A glass house for plants needing protection from the weather is a .....
6. We like living ..... the country.

Time to check your answers. If you made too many mistakes, there's no need to feel *distress* or to *whine;* just do the difficult questions again!

Key

I 1a, 2b, 3b, 4b, 5c, 6a, 7b, 8c

II 1c, 2c, 3b, 4a, 5b, 6a, 7b, 8c, 9c, 10b

III 1a, 2c, 3c, 4b, 5c, 6b, 7b, 8a, 9c, 10c

IV 1T, 2F, 3T, 4F, 5T, 6T, 7F, 8F, 9T, 10F (*alternative spelling:* hooves), 11F, 12T, 13T, 14T, 15T, 16T, 17F, 18T, 19F, 20T, 21F, 22F

V 1f, 2g, 3c, 4e, 5h, 6a, 7b, 8i, 9d

VI 1d, 2e, 3b, 4a, 5f, 6c, 7i, 8h, 9g, 10k, 11j

VII 1 landowner, 2 barn, 3 dogs, 4 shepherd, 5 gardener, 6 vines, 7 flower-shop, 8 plantation

VIII 1 make, 2 can't, 3 left, 4 give (send; "make" here would mean "weave", "knit", "build", etc.), 5 bite, 6 mow, 7 smell (are), 8 Make

IX 1 in, 2 from ... to, 3 in, 4 to, 5 of, 6 of, 7 at, 8 for, 9 of

X 1 on, 2 beds (pots), 3 by, 4 in, 5 greenhouse (hothouse), 6 in

How many mistakes have you made?

	I to VI	VII to IX	X
Excellent	0— 3	0— 2	0 mistakes
Good	4— 7	3— 4	1 mistakes
Satisfactory	8—12	5— 6	2 mistakes
Not very good	13—18	7—11	3 mistakes
Weak	over 18	over 11	over 3 mistakes

Chapter X Transportation and Communication

It's fun to go to a foreign country, stand around, look at the *statues* and *monuments*, *wander* into *museums* and *wander* out again, get something to eat and *get* totally *lost*. That's easy! But sometimes it's important to be able to say, "Where's the *left-luggage office?*" or, "My *windscreen* is broken; where can I get a new one?" or, "Put down that gun, you fool! This plane doesn't have enough petrol for a *non-stop flight* to Libya!"

Therefore we've written this chapter for you on *means of transportation and communication:* this includes *postal* services, wheeled *vehicles*, *sea-going* ships, and *air-sick* passengers.

I. What's the opposite?

1. Where's the timetable for *departures* and
   a) arrivals?
   b) trains leaving?
   c) opening times?

2. The train *pulled in* at 9 o'clock and
   a) overturned at 9:30.
   b) got in at 9:30.
   c) left at 9:30.

3. From Rome to Milan the train was *crowded*, but after Milan it was
   a) fast.
   b) pleasant.
   c) empty.

4. "Excuse me. Is this seat *reserved* or
   a) free?"
   b) taken?"
   c) occupied?"

5. The *prudent* father refused to buy a new car for his
   a) inexperienced son.
   b) immoral son.
   c) reckless son.

6. I enjoyed the *take-off* more than
   a) the loading.
   b) the landing.
   c) taking it on.

7. In Frankfurt I *caught the connection*, but in Munich I
   a) dropped it.
   b) sent it back.
   c) missed it.

8. We *docked* in Plymouth and two weeks later we
   a) put to sea.
   b) rode at anchor.
   c) reached port.

9. He explored both the *interior* and the
   a) front.
   b) coast.
   c) area out of town.

10. Lake Geneva is *renowned* for its beauty, but Lake Mariensee is
   a) out of fashion.
   b) little known.
   c) not crowded.

11. On business trips he was always *animated*, but at home with his wife he was
   a) civilized.
   b) discouraging.
   c) dull.

12. Our family moved from the *suburbs* to the
   a) centre of town.
   b) surrounding area.
   c) mountains.

13. The post-office clerk said, "Please print the *addressee* and the
   a) sender clearly."
   b) receiver clearly."
   c) name clearly."

II. Which word or phrase has almost the same meaning?

1. "I'm new here. How do you make a *local call* from this telephone?"
   a) within the same company or building
   b) within the city or town
   c) outside the city or town

2. I'd like to *wire* a message to Chicago.
   a) ask for
   b) telephone
   c) cable

3. He may have moved, so write "*Please forward*" on the envelope.
   a) send to his new address
   b) hold for him
   c) return to the sender

4. The fastest way to get around London is by *tube*.
   a) taxi
   b) bus
   c) underground

5. Be careful of the *pedestrians!*
   a) slow drivers
   b) people on foot
   c) small, loose stones on the road

6. The railway is now offering *reduced fares* on Sundays.
   a) cheaper round-trip tickets
   b) lowered prices
   c) small meals included in the price of a ticket

7. Do you think the train will have a *sleeping-car?*
   a) bed
   b) compartment with beds
   c) carriage with beds

8. "I'm sorry. These seats are *taken*."
   a) sold
   b) reserved
   c) removed for repairs

9. The girls *smashed* the glass.
   a) cleaned
   b) cut
   c) broke to pieces

10. The *collision* killed three persons, two dogs and a cow.
    a) fight
    b) crash
    c) vehicle

11. You just can't depend on those *trawlers!*
    a) electric buses
    b) fishing boats
    c) very slow trains

12. Let's take a *ferry!*
    a) trip by boat
    b) ride without paying
    c) boat to carry people and cars across a river, channel, etc.

13. We *embarked* at Ostend for Dover.
    a) landed at Ostend instead of Dover
    b) arrived at Ostend from Dover
    c) got on a ship going from Ostend to Dover

14. The crossing was *tempestuous*.
    a) stormy
    b) short
    c) fast

15. My son thought the *tempest* was exciting.
    a) violent storm
    b) short sea voyage
    c) small, fast boat

16. "Captain, watch out! She's going to be *sea-sick!*"
    a) to jump over the side
    b) to collide with something
    c) to be sick from the ship's motion

17. The sea crashed noisily against the *bow*.
    a) front part of a ship
    b) back part of a ship
    c) lower decks

18. Many little *leaks* can sink a big ship.
    a) underwater rocks
    b) holes which let in water
    c) errors in navigation

19. When his *glider* crashed he broke his arm.
a) private plane
b) plane without an engine
c) plane which can land on water

20. I saw the planes *collide* in mid-air!
a) refuel
b) explode
c) crash into each other

21. The *fuselage* is burning.
a) fuel for a plane
b) body of a plane
c) luggage compartment

III. Which choice makes sense?

1. Our mailbox is usually
a) emptied at noon.
b) taken away at noon.
c) sent at noon.

2. The postmark
a) cost more than I had expected.
b) said "registered letter".
c) proves it was mailed on Friday.

3. I sent him a postal order
a) requesting 500 stamps.
b) for his birthday.
c) telling them to forward my mail.

4. He sent his mother a postcard
a) for £ 50.
b) with $5 inside.
c) so the postman could read his jokes, too.

5. The compartment
a) was empty.
b) waved his hand.
c) read, "from London, 9:35".

6. A timetable
a) tells the time in various cities.
b) lists opening and closing times.
c) lists arrivals and departures.

7. In 1861 English engineers proposed a tunnel
a) under the English Channel.
b) over the London railway tracks.
c) from Paris to Berlin.

8. Strong barriers
a) lit up the tracks at night.
b) rode as guards on the trains.
c) kept the people off the tracks.

9. We flew from Frankfurt to Los Angeles, with stopovers
a) served hot by the stewardesses.
b) in London and New York.
c) in the air.

10. The pilot made a forced landing because
a) the plane was 40 minutes late.
b) the runway was wet.
c) we ran out of fuel.

11. The lighthouses
a) were closed by the city police.
b) control the take-offs and landings of planes.
c) are visible for miles.

12. Pilots
a) guide ships into ports.
b) drive locomotives.
c) load and unload planes.

13. "The number is engaged.
a) It's reserved from here to Oslo."
b) The next flight leaves at noon."
c) Could you call back later?"

14. He pulled on the oars
a) to call the steward.
b) and the train stopped abruptly.
c) and the boat began to move.

15. The visibility
a) needed cleaning.
b) was about 4 kilometres.
c) tied up at the docks.

16. The old crew
a) joked about the officers.
b) needed repairs badly.
c) was 45 hours.

17. The anchor
a) has been lowered.
b) is burning!
c) is full of people.

18. I haven't got my sea-legs yet,
a) so I'll have to borrow yours.
b) so I don't know where we are.
c) so I'm going to be sick.

19. The car overtook
a) the road.
b) the front.
c) the lorry.

20. The paths in the park were paved with
a) green benches.
b) red bricks.
c) flower-sellers.

21. He used the suitcase to
a) carry his gun collection.
b) iron his wife's dress.
c) punch the passenger's ticket.

Did you know that the language of international *air-traffic* is English? It's true. *Pilots* of international *airliners* usually use English when they talk over the radio to the ground control stations.

IV. Is it true or false?

		T	F
1.	A passenger train is faster than an express train.	☐	☐
2.	A freight train is a train with a damaged locomotive.	☐	☐
3.	A goods train is fast and very comfortable for passengers.	☐	☐
4.	In a train you can put your suitcases on the luggage rack.	☐	☐
5.	A scooter is larger and faster than a motor-cycle.	☐	☐
6.	A cyclist is a motorist who drives round and round in circles.	☐	☐
7.	There is heavy traffic during the rush hour.	☐	☐
8.	Almost every new car in Europe has lifebelts.	☐	☐
9.	You can see a headlight shining and hear a horn honking.	☐	☐
10.	A traffic signal has red, orange and green lights, to direct the flow of traffic.	☐	☐
11.	Traffic lights and traffic signs are set up to prevent traffic accidents.	☐	☐
12.	You can park your car in a parking lot.	☐	☐
13.	A repair-shop overhauls cars.	☐	☐
14.	A detour is a trip home after having visited museums, monuments and other places of interest.	☐	☐
15.	A fare is a gathering of people, held regularly, to show, buy and sell things.	☐	☐
16.	A fountain is often used for writing letters and postcards.	☐	☐
17.	A life-boat is a small boat used for pleasure.	☐	☐
18.	Passengers on ships sleep in cabins.	☐	☐
19.	A shipwreck is a sailor who was seriously injured while at sea.	☐	☐
20.	Boats cannot travel on a navigable river.	☐	☐
21.	A deck is a small blanket used by travellers, especially on ships and planes.	☐	☐
22.	An airliner is a large plane for carrying passengers, usually over long distances.	☐	☐
23.	In general, jet planes are slower than propeller-driven planes.	☐	☐
24.	A helicopter can take off and land without a runway.	☐	☐
25.	The cockpit is the part of the plane where the pilot sits.	☐	☐
26.	The job of a telephone operator is to repair telephones.	☐	☐

V. Find the nouns which go together.

1. windscreen
2. car
3. lorry
4. driver
5. cab
6. service station
7. motorway
8. tyres

a) gas station, b) windshield, c) truck, d) wheels, e) taxi, f) automobile, g) highway, h) motorist

9. pavement
10. environs
11. skyscraper
12. statue
13. tram

i) tall building, j) streetcar, k) surroundings, l) monument, m) sidewalk

14. booking-office
15. luggage van
16. engine
17. junction
18. rails
19. underground

n) meeting point, o) baggage car, p) subway, q) ticket office, r) tracks, s) locomotive

VI. Find the words which go together.

1. to cable .....
2. to pump up .....
3. to dim .....
4. to overhaul .....
5. to honk .....

a) an engine, b) a tyre, c) the horn, d) a message, e) the headlights

6. to take leave .....
7. to ferry .....
8. to hover .....
9. to be run over .....
10. to change .....

f) into second gear, g) over an area, h) by a car, i) of a friend, j) across a river

11. ticket-.....
12. express .....
13. dining-.....
14. emergency .....

k) train, l) brake, m) collector, n) car

15. road .....
16. speed-.....
17. spare .....
18. filling .....
19. reverse .....

o) limit, p) station, q) gear, r) sign, s) parts

VII. Put in the right noun.

1. He carefully signed the letter, folded it, and put it in the .....
2. "I'm sorry, there is no Mr Jones here. You have the wrong ....."
3. The train to London leaves from ..... number three.
4. In a train station, a ..... carries passengers' luggage.
5. "Attach no stamps. ..... will be paid by addressee."
6. If you want to register this letter, you'll have to take it to the .....
7. We just got a letter from George! He must have wanted us to get it quickly, because he sent it .....
8. She always writes her letters on blue .....
9. If you don't know his number, look it up in the telephone .....
10. The letters P.O.B. stand for .....
11. The letters C.O.D. stand for .....
12. If you have to send him that contract, send it as a registered .....
13. Books, newspapers and magazines can be sent cheaply, as printed .....
14. Ships can be loaded, unloaded, repaired or built in .....
15. He's a salesman in a clothing store, but he dreams of being the ..... of an airliner.
16. My non-stop ..... from Amsterdam to Zurich was faster than the bus ride from Zurich airport to the centre of the city.
17. Modern jets travel at supersonic .....

VIII. Put in the right verb.

1. If you don't know the streets, it's very easy to ..... lost in London.
2. We have plenty of time and the weather is beautiful. Let's just ..... about for a while.
3. The sign said: "..... off the grass".
4. "I want to be absolutely certain this letter arrives, so when you post it, please ..... it."
5. The mail came just this minute. Would you like to ..... it?
6. The postman drove from pillar-box to pillar-box, ... the letters.
7. "Mr White is talking on another telephone. ..... the line, please."
8. I'll be arriving at 6 o'clock tonight. Can you ..... me at the station?
9. The train ..... ten minutes late.
10. "Watch out! Stop! Oh no! You just ..... through a red light!"
11. When the driver saw the cow on the tracks, he ..... the brakes immediately, but it was too late.
12. It was a terrible winter for driving! About twenty different times I ..... on ice!

13. As soon as I saw their car ..... with the train, I knew it was hopeless.
14. Would you rather walk or ..... a bus?

IX. Put in the right adjective, adverb or preposition.

1. We sent you the bill ..... post.
2. Could you take this letter ..... the post-office for me, please?
3. Some of these letters will be delivered, and the others will be called .....
4. I couldn't reach you by phone today. The line was out ..... order.
5. "I'm sorry, sir; we can't put ..... your call to London. All the lines are busy."
6. My 15-year-old daughter loves to talk ..... the phone.
7. Would you like to go ..... the seaside on Sunday?
8. The President said, "Our nation shall defend the freedom ..... the seas!"
9. The ship calls ..... New York once a month.
10. He was ..... the wheel when the accident happened.
11. We had to tow the car ..... the nearest garage.
12. He was so drunk that he ran his car ..... a brick wall.
13. My dog was run ..... by a car.
14. Last night someone stole the tyres from the front wheels, but left them on the ..... wheels.
15. We sent the parcels ..... train.
16. We stopped over for an hour ..... London.

X. Review: Put in the right word.

1. The postman empties the ..... every day at 4 p.m.
2. We embarked at New York ..... Helsinki.
3. The car in front of us went so slowly that I had to ..... into second gear.
4. The old man ferried us ..... the river.
5. When you are on a train, you can buy a meal in the .....-car.
6. The train pulled ..... at 9 o'clock.
7. You can't drive down this street; it's a one-..... street.

You can check your answers now; we hope the results aren't *tragic!*

Key

I 1a, 2c, 3c, 4a, 5c, 6b, 7c, 8a, 9b, 10b, 11c, 12a, 13a

II 1b, 2c, 3a, 4c, 5b, 6b, 7c, 8b, 9c, 10b, 11b, 12c, 13c, 14a, 15a, 16c, 17a, 18b, 19b, 20c, 21b

III 1a, 2c, 3b, 4c, 5a, 6c, 7a, 8c, 9b, 10c, 11c, 12a, 13c, 14c, 15b, 16a, 17a, 18c, 19c, 20b, 21a

IV 1F, 2F, 3F, 4T, 5F, 6F, 7T, 8F (cars have *seat-belts*), 9T, 10T, 11T, 12T, 13T, 14F, 15F (*notice:* fare, fair), 16F, 17F, 18T, 19F, 20F, 21F, 22T, 23F, 24T, 25T, 26F

V 1b, 2f, 3c, 4h, 5e, 6a, 7g, 8d, 9m, 10k, 11i, 12l, 13j, 14q, 15o, 16s, 17n, 18r, 19p

VI 1d, 2b, 3e, 4a, 5c, 6i, 7j, 8g, 9h, 10f, 11m, 12k, 13n, 14l, 15r, 16o, 17s, 18p, 19q

VII 1 envelope, 2 number, 3 platform, 4 porter, 5 Postage, 6 post-office, 7 special delivery (express), 8 stationery (note-paper), 9 directory, 10 post-office box, 11 cash on delivery, 12 letter, 13 matter, 14 docks, 15 pilot, 16 flight, 17 speed(s)

VIII 1 get, 2 wander (walk), 3 Keep, 4 register, 5 open (see, look at), 6 collecting, 7 Hold, 8 meet, 9 is (was, arrived, came (in), got in, left), 10 went (drove, *Am* ran), 11 applied (put on), 12 skidded, 13 collide, 14 take (go by)

IX 1 by, 2 to, 3 for, 4 of, 5 through, 6 on, 7 to, 8 of, 9 at, 10 at (behind), 11 to, 12 into, 13 over, 14 rear (back), 15 by, 16 in

X 1 letter-box (pillar-box, *Am* mailbox), 2 for, 3 change, 4 across, 5 dining, 6 out (in), 7 way

How many mistakes have you made?

	I to VI	VII to IX	X
Excellent	0— 6	0— 5	0 mistakes
Good	7—12	6—10	1 mistakes
Satisfactory	13—20	11—16	2 mistakes
Not very good	21—29	17—24	3 mistakes
Weak	over 29	over 24	over 3 mistakes

Chapter XI Sport

If you're like most people, every once in a while you'll feel a powerful desire to set your books on fire and get out of the house. But what do you do once you're free? Do you *go in for sport?* Do you like to *sprint* to the nearest *tennis-court* and hit a few *tennis-balls*, or disappear into the woods, *pitch a tent* and *go fishing?*

It's fun to do some *physical* exercise — like *skating* or *skiing* — but don't forget to keep a balance. As the ancient Romans said, "A healthy brain in a healthy body." Your mind needs *gymnastics* just as your body does.

I. What's the opposite?

1. "He's not bad at tennis, but I'd rather have him as my *opponent* than as my
   a) partner."
   b) trainer."
   c) student."
2. You're a fool if you think this *amateur* will beat that
   a) unpopular player.
   b) professional.
   c) cheater.
3. When I was young my body was *flexible*, but now I feel
   a) out of practice.
   b) stiff.
   c) strong.
4. I'd rather play with a *sportsmanlike* player than with one who is
   a) too clever.
   b) weak and unhealthy.
   c) unfair.
5. Every race has a *winner* and at least one
   a) challenger.
   b) loser.
   c) obstacle.
6. He's won prizes for *sprinting*, but he's hopeless at
   a) pacing.
   b) long-distance running.
   c) serious, professional events.

II. Which word or phrase has almost the same meaning?

1. She talks about nothing but *athletics*.
   a) sports heroes
   b) running, jumping, etc.
   c) very strong men
2. A good sportsman needs a *supple* body.
   a) healthy and well-trained
   b) strong and flexible
   c) active

3. Let's go to the *gymnasium!*
   a) teacher or trainer for sports
   b) school, especially for sports
   c) room or hall for sports

4. He *beat the record.*
   a) hit the record
   b) set a new record
   c) attacked the record-holder

5. My horse is *trailing* again, of course.
   a) breathing hard
   b) ahead of the other horses
   c) behind the other horses

6. "For me, killing foxes is less interesting than the *pursuit.*"
   a) chase
   b) excitement
   c) reward

III. Which choice makes sense?

1. Do you like to go camping
   a) for a cup?
   b) for applause?
   c) with your wife?

2. Where can we buy canvas
   a) containers for liquids?
   b) food?
   c) tents?

3. Our teacher was famous for his physical
   a) strength.
   b) prizes.
   c) knowledge.

4. The contest
   a) was three to one.
   b) ended in a draw.
   c) landed five metres away.

5. We challenged
   a) their golf course.
   b) his sports club.
   c) our physical training.

6. They kicked off
   a) the referee's teeth.
   b) and started the game.
   c) until the final whistle.

7. He passed the
   a) game.
   b) ball.
   c) cheers.

8. Umpires
   a) support the team.
   b) keep the sports grounds clean.
   c) decide what is fair.

Learning a foreign language is like running a *long-distance race:* you need steady effort over a long period of time.

IV. Is it true or false?

		T	F
1.	In a stadium, spectators sit in the grandstand.	☐	☐
2.	A horse-race is a sports event.	☐	☐
3.	Most people skate on snow and ski on ice.	☐	☐
4.	A goalkeeper, a forward and a referee are members of a football team.	☐	☐
5.	A steeplechase is a race in which dogs chase a mechanical rabbit.	☐	☐
6.	In a boxing-match, two men wrestle each other.	☐	☐
7.	Fresh-water fish live in rivers and lakes, salt-water fish in the ocean.	☐	☐
8	Big game hunters hunt pheasants.	☐	☐

V. Find the nouns which go together.

1. trainer
2. umpire
3. caravan
4. angler
5. bait
6. cheers

a) worms, b) trailer, c) coach, d) referee, e) applause, f) fisherman

VI. Find the words which go together.

1. football .....
2. golf-.....
3. tennis-.....
4. high .....
5. weight-.....
6. boat-.....
7. race-.....

a) lifting, b) court, c) jump, d) horse, e) links, f) field, g) race

VII. Put in the right noun.

1. "What's the .....?" — "Three goals to one."
2. The referee blew the final .....
3. The runner who breaks the ..... wins the race.
4. He holds the world ..... in the long jump.
5. When did Muhammad Ali become the world ..... heavyweight boxer?
6. We can't play football today; the ..... is closed because it's too wet.

VIII. Put in the right verb.

1. This is a good place to camp! Let's ..... our tent here.
2. This was a good camping trip, but it's time to ..... the tent and go home.
3. I heard you ..... fishing yesterday! Did you ..... a good catch?
4. Who ..... that goal?
5. I can ..... the discus farther than you can!
6. When the spectators heard he had just set a new world record, they ..... wildly.
7. Is it more important to win or to ..... fair?
8. He knows he won't win, but he doesn't care; he just wants to ..... a good race.
9. His father is wealthy enough to ..... a racing stable.

IX. Put in the right adverb or preposition.

1. My brother is rather fond ..... sport, but I'm afraid I don't really go in ..... sport very much.
2. "Your son likes to race ..... his friends, because he usually wins."
3. Kick-off will be ..... 2:30 p.m.
4. "Number 6 is ..... an offside position!"
5. "The centre-forward had a clear shot ..... the goal, but he missed!"
6. What was the score ..... half-time?
7. Is it too early to take ..... a fishing-licence for the season?
8. The fisherman threw his line ..... the water, sat down on the bank, and waited peacefully ..... a bite.
9. He hooked a fish and quickly hauled it .....
10. As soon as the wild geese heard us, they flew .....

X. Review: Put in the right word.

1. The game ended ..... a draw.
2. We won't be able to play tennis today; all the tennis-..... are taken.
3. The game will start in a few seconds. The players are getting ready to kick .....
4. Fresh-..... fish live in rivers and lakes.
5. Big ..... hunters hunt bears and lions.
6. The angler put the ..... on the hook and threw the line into the water.
7. "Come on! Let's run down to the football ..... and kick a ball around!"
8. A professional plays a sport for money, but an ..... does not.

Check your answers and find out your *score!* How well did you do?

Key

I 1a, 2b, 3b, 4c, 5b, 6b

II 1b, 2b, 3c, 4b, 5c, 6a

III 1c, 2c, 3a, 4b, 5b, 6b, 7b, 8c

IV 1T, 2T, 3F, 4F, 5F, 6F, 7T, 8F

V 1c, 2d, 3b, 4f, 5a, 6e

VI 1f, 2e, 3b, 4c, 5a, 6g, 7d

VII 1 score, 2 whistle, 3 tape, 4 record, 5 champion, 6 football field (sports ground, playground)

VIII 1 pitch (put up), 2 strike (take down), 3 went ... make, 4 scored *(football)* / kicked *(Rugby)*, 5 throw, 6 applauded (cheered), 7 play, 8 run, 9 keep (own)

IX 1 of ... for, 2 against (with), 3 at, 4 in, 5 at, 6 at, 7 out, 8 into ... for, 9 in, 10 away (off)

X 1 in, 2 courts, 3 off, 4 water, 5 game, 6 bait, 7 field, 8 amateur

How many mistakes have you made?

	I to VI	VII to IX	X
Excellent	0— 2	0— 2	0 mistakes
Good	3— 4	3— 5	1 mistakes
Satisfactory	5— 7	6— 9	2 mistakes
Not very good	8—10	10—13	3 mistakes
Weak	over 10	over 13	over 3 mistakes

Chapter XII Science, Literature, Education

In the past three years we've visited Switzerland, Sweden, Norway, Hungary, West Germany and Japan. In every one of these countries we met *scientists* and *scholars*, especially in the fields of *philosophy*, history, *mathematics*, *chemistry*, *physics* and medicine. Almost all the *researchers* and *professors* we met had *published* at least one *essay* or scientific *treatise* in English, because, as one *writer* told us, "Anyone who *does research work* can simply *exercise a greater influence* by writing in English."

If you hope to share in the *intellectual* developments outside your own country, either by reading about them or *publishing* some *papers* yourself, you'll find English useful.

I. What's the opposite?

1. In this case, the *exception* proves the
   a) example.
   b) rule.
   c) result.

2. It's a good idea in *theory*, but I wonder how it will work in
   a) practice.
   b) a survey.
   c) a text.

3. *Well-founded* theories are generally more attractive than
   a) lost ones.
   b) unfounded ones.
   c) very intellectual ones.

4. It's not safe to *ignore* this problem. It would be better to
   a) pay attention to it.
   b) know a lot about it.
   c) appear to be clever.

5. I've seen him act in both *tragedies* and
   a) comedies.
   b) films.
   c) on the stage.

6. He said, "John Lilly wrote in an *elaborate* style, Ernest Hemingway in
   a) a natural style."
   b) a simple style."
   c) a realistic style."

7. Some political leaders prefer to give *obscure* answers rather than
   a) honest ones.
   b) detailed ones.
   c) clear ones.

8. The bad books he wrote are *tedious*, but the good ones are
   a) immortal.
   b) fascinating.
   c) simple, moral stories.

9. The boy has such a strong *imagination* that he pays little attention to
   a) his insufficiencies.
   b) morality.
   c) facts.

10. The *nobility* fought bitterly against
   a) evil.
   b) the common people.
   c) the aristocrats.

11. The *peaceful* period from 1871 to 1914 was followed by
   a) a violent one.
   b) a terrible one.
   c) an interesting one.

12. T. S. Eliot wrote both *prose* and
   a) novels.
   b) essays.
   c) poetry.

13. You can only *criticize!* Why don't you ever try to
   a) think before you talk?
   b) be specific?
   c) praise me?

14. Anything you could do now would only *complicate* the problem rather than
   a) make it interesting.
   b) make it simpler.
   c) make it worse.

15. "Will the test be *oral* or
   a) difficult?"
   b) written?"
   c) easy?"

Do you agree with Sir Richard Steele (1710)?

"*Reading* is to the mind what exercise is to the body."

II. Which word or phrase has almost the same meaning?

1. She won a *scholarship* to Oxford.
   a) admission to Oxford
   b) money for studying at Oxford
   c) prize for achievement at Oxford

2. He's a man of considerable *culture.*
   a) imagination
   b) intelligence
   c) learning and artistic taste

3. They studied the *culture* of ancient Peru.
   a) history
   b) activities of its cultured men
   c) customs, art, civilization, etc.

4. A *learned* man is a
   a) skilful teacher.
   b) man of great knowledge.
   c) man who has gone to school.

5. The science teacher said, "It takes a good mind to find the *obvious* answer."
   a) hidden but correct
   b) deep and requiring thought
   c) clear and easily understood

6. I *distinctly* heard him say, "No."
   a) clearly
   b) firmly
   c) definitely

7. "I've never met anyone with better manners or worse *morals*."
   a) common sense
   b) ability to think
   c) principles which guide behaviour

8. I don't want to *contemplate* the results.
   a) discuss
   b) think about
   c) become confused about

9. This child will be my *downfall!*
   a) cause of ruin
   b) cause of being fooled
   c) reason for losing money

10. The nation was *compelled* to defend itself.
    a) led
    b) forced
    c) persuaded

11. His *verses* won the college prize.
    a) essays on literature
    b) poems or lines from poems
    c) students from the opposite group

12. His *poetic* efforts were terrible.
    a) efforts to write verse
    b) efforts to write fiction
    c) efforts to write novels

13. We lost the *copyright*.
    a) right to publish a book
    b) right to copy a book
    c) final copy of an unprinted work

14. Edmund Spenser is famous for his *melodious* poetry.
    a) evil
    b) sounding like a sweet melody
    c) extremely sad, empty of all joy

15. His style of writing is definitely *affected*.
    a) false and unnatural
    b) expressive and powerful
    c) strongly influenced by other writers

16. This chapter may be *omitted*.
    a) left out
    b) torn out
    c) sent away

17. "You'll have to take a *proficiency* exam, I'm afraid."
    a) test to become a professional
    b) test showing the level of skill or knowledge
    c) test for admission to a university

18. "Your son is very *attentive*. I often notice that he
    a) gets himself into trouble."
    b) makes other children laugh."
    c) observes things carefully."

19. Charles Darwin wrote that man *evolved* from monkey-like creatures.
    a) took land from
    b) developed from
    c) learned from

20 They always use the same *procedure*.
    a) very uninteresting approach
    b) very complicated process
    c) method

Do you agree with Dale or with Tennyson?

"There may be *morality* where there is no religion; but that there should be religion where there is no *morality*, is impossible."
R. W. Dale (1878)

"Evil must come upon us headlong, if *morality* tries to get on without religion."
Alfred Lord Tennyson (1897)

III. Which choice makes sense?

1. A very high level of civilization was reached by
    a) mountain climbers.
    b) scientists at the North Pole.
    c) the ancient Greeks.

2. He was well rewarded for his exploration of
    a) bombs.
    b) northwest Africa.
    c) scientific demonstrations.

3. The results of the experiment confirmed
    a) my expectations.
    b) the extension.
    c) the exercise.

4. He proceeded
    a) me.
    b) the test.
    c) to explain the problem.

5. Do you believe that the end justifies	a) the means? b) the middle? c) the goal?
6. Men of the Stone Age	a) were made of stone. b) made tools of stone. c) weigh over 112 kilograms.
7. His conversation is always formal,	a) stiff and precise. b) warm and friendly. c) like a child.
8. He spends hours cleaning his antiques and	a) uncles. b) old pictures. c) his other insects.
9. The students' essays	a) were badly written. b) were badly painted. c) went home early.
10. The comments	a) print stories and pictures. b) appeared with the text. c) lived in the same house.
11. I gave her a summary	a) as a reward. b) as a punishment. c) of the book.
12. It's a little volume but a great	a) man. b) book. c) quantity.
13. The author wrote, "This book is dedicated	a) by heart." b) ahead." c) to them."
14. Your essay is good, but there is an important omission:	a) you wrote too much. b) you spelt several words wrong. c) you didn't discuss the causes.
15. You can skip this chapter; really,	a) I don't need the book any more. b) it's easy to understand. c) don't bother to read it.
16. The book is composed of	a) a skilful editor. b) a well-known author. c) 25 well-organized chapters.
17. It's difficult to understand the teacher's dictations because	a) he knows that I like him. b) his pronunciation is so bad. c) his handwriting is so bad.

18. The young girls recited
   a) the class.
   b) their poems.
   c) the older students

19. He was a diligent student,
   a) studying day and night.
   b) so of course he failed the test.
   c) so he finished his essays late.

20. My son is playing truant
   a) in the school play.
   b) in the school band.
   c) from school today.

Do you agree ?

"Justice, truth, love, duty, virtue — in one word, *morality*."
E. R. Conder (1877)

IV. Is it true or false?

		T	F
1.	A duke's wife is a duchess.	☐	☐
2.	A monarch rules in a monarchy.	☐	☐
3.	A treatise is an agreement between two or more nations.	☐	☐
4.	Good scientists cannot ignore the need for precision.	☐	☐
5.	A witty man is feeble-minded.	☐	☐
6.	The USA has fought many wars, but never a civil war.	☐	☐
7.	All living persons are immortal.	☐	☐
8.	The United Nations is an international organization.	☐	☐
9.	A rhyme is a long story, usually a poem.	☐	☐
10.	Novels and short stories are works of fiction.	☐	☐
11.	A proverb is a verb which stands for another verb.	☐	☐
12.	A dictionary explains the meanings of words.	☐	☐
13.	An editor prepares books for publication.	☐	☐
14.	Shakespeare's works have been printed in many editions.	☐	☐
15.	Most paragraphs consist of more than one chapter.	☐	☐
16.	Most ceremonies are intended to have comic effects.	☐	☐
17.	Most of the children in England attend public schools.	☐	☐
18.	The headmaster supervises the work of the teaching staff.	☐	☐

Do you agree ?

"*International* law is the limit and conscience of the strongest."
The Times (London, about 1872)

V. Find the nouns which go together.

1. preface
2. conviction
3. illusion
4. utility
5. notion
6. author

a) usefulness, b) foreword, c) idea, d) mistake, e) writer, f) certainty

7. break
8. teaching staff
9. headmaster
10. composition
11. school-grounds
12. satchel

g) recess, h) schoolbag, i) essay, j) faculty, k) campus, l) principal

13. geography
14. geometry
15. arithmetic
16. research
17. civics
18. literature
19. biology

m) government, n) land, o) circles and squares, p) poetry, q) numbers, r) investigation, s) life

VI. Find the words which go together.

1. short .....
2. ballpoint-.....
3. boarding .....
4. table of .....

a) contents, b) story, c) school, d) pen

5. a quotation .....
6. all imaginable .....
7. a keen .....
8. a historical .....

e) mind, f) possibilities, g) event, h) from Shakespeare

9. What gives you ..... ?
10. You needn't .....
11. That happens .....
12. It caused a .....
13. Whose turn ..... ?

i) sometimes, j) that idea, k) is it, l) justify yourself, m) sensation

Do you agree?

"Wealth commands the ear of *greatness*."
Dr. Samuel Johnson (1751)

"It is the mystery surrounding great men which gives them their *greatness*."
Washington Irving (1809; the *quotation* is *edited* slightly)

VII. Put in the right noun.

1. "Geese" is the ..... of "goose".
2. "Goose" is the ..... of "geese".
3. Albert Einstein was a famous .....
4. A ..... studies, teaches or writes about history.
5. Charles Darwin's theory of ..... is the basis of modern biology.
6. A king's son is a .....
7. A king's daughter is a .....
8. An emperor's wife is an .....
9. The usual ..... for the word "verb" is "vb".
10. A ..... is in charge of an elementary school or a secondary school.
11. After leaving secondary school, he continued his ..... at university.
12. The English language has a ..... of about 500,000 words.
13. The letters "a", "e", "i", "o", "u" are ....., and the letters "b", "c", "d", "f", "g", etc. are .....
14. In the word "cheerful", the ..... is on "cheer-", not on "-ful".
15. A sign consisting of two points, one placed above the other, like this (:), is called a .....
16. A sign consisting of a point placed above a comma, like this (;), is called a .....
17. A sign consisting of a small straight line above a point, like this (!), is called an .....
18. Signs which indicate a quotation and look like this (" ") are called .....
19. A sign which is a short line like this (—) and which separates some words from the rest of a sentence — like this — is called a .....
20. The sign which looks like this (') and is usually used to indicate possession, as in "the girl's big toe", is called an .....
21. (The curved lines at the beginning and end of this sentence indicate that the entire sentence is in .....)
22. If you fail the entrance ....., you won't be able to go to this school.
23. "I don't like my teacher," the girl said. "I don't like to work at home in the evenings and he gives too much ....."
24. Is it "conveni<u>e</u>nce" or "conveni<u>a</u>nce"? I was always bad at .....
25. Immediately after he received his degree, he began teaching at an American university, as a ..... of physics.

Do you agree?

"Pleasure by itself is *insufficient.*"

VIII. Put in the right verb.

1. Have you ..... any conclusions yet?
2. "A very interesting experiment. And what conclusions did you ..... from it?"
3. He's a good researcher. When he attacks a problem he ..... a thorough investigation.
4. I like working with him, because he ..... such a keen mind.
5. Why don't you ..... your common sense?
6. The rumour ..... like wildfire.
7. Did you ..... the exam?
8. I don't know. I haven't ..... an opinion about it yet.
9. He ..... absolutely no conception of what we're doing.
10. When his book first came out, most of the newspapers ..... it favourably.
11. Johnny drew a line under a word, so he would remember it, but the teacher asked him, "Why did you ..... that word?"
12. Do you like to ..... gymnastics in school?
13. At our school tuition ..... free.
14. He's a good teacher, but he usually ..... his lectures at 7:30 in the morning, and I just refuse to ..... a lecture that early.
15. The chemistry teacher is excellent. I'm only sorry that he isn't allowed to ..... private lessons.
16. "Take out a sheet of paper, boys," the teacher said cheerfully. "It's time for you to ..... a dictation."

IX. Put in the right adjective or preposition.

1. It just occurs ..... me that the word "sole" is pronounced the same as "soul".
2. Your plan is excellent ..... theory, but I know ..... experience that it won't work.
3. Isaac Newton's theory has exercised an extremely strong influence ..... scientists.
4. He believes a scholar should never deviate ..... the truth.
5. He went ..... school in Manchester.
6. He's an expert ..... his field, but he's ignorant ..... the simplest facts of daily life.
7. What proof can you offer ..... support of your statement?
8. ..... careful consideration, we've decided against accepting your essay for publication.
9. "There's the bell, boys. The test is over. It's time to hand ..... your test papers."
10. "I'd like to make a study ..... Goethe's early years."

11. "In this case," said the professor, "I'm rather unwilling to depart ..... long-established tradition."
12. Plato and Aristotle are great figures of ..... culture, and Virgil and Julius Caesar of ..... culture.
13. "When you write, you put too many sentences ..... parentheses."
14. "You know, you've been commenting pretty freely ..... all our mistakes."
15. We won't be able to get the book from the publisher any more. It's out ..... print.
16. Have you posted your application ..... admission yet?
17. "Why did the teacher keep you ..... after school today? Was he angry with you?"
18. The children aren't home yet. They're still ..... school.
19. He asked his mathematics teacher, "Would it be possible to have private lessons .... you?"
20. "I hear your daughter is studying ..... a university."

X. Review: Put in the right word.

1. For her civics class she wrote an excellent ..... on Willy Brandt.
2. I just don't believe that the end ..... the means.
3. He's a good man for ..... research work.
4. The book is badly organized and has no table ..... contents.
5. The professor hopes to ..... an influence on the decisions of the committee.
6. Did you take my ballpoint-..... ?
7. A semi-colon consists of a point placed above a ....., like this (;).
8. Did you know that the ..... of the word "soul" is the same as that of the word "sole"?

Now you can check your answers, *underline* all the words you didn't know, and take a *break*. But don't forget to do your *homework*, which is to study your mistakes!

Key

I 1b, 2a, 3b, 4a, 5a, 6b, 7c, 8b, 9c, 10b, 11a, 12c, 13c, 14b, 15b

II 1b, 2c, 3c, 4b, 5c, 6a, 7c, 8b, 9a, 10b, 11b, 12a, 13a, 14b, 15a, 16a, 17b, 18c, 19b, 20c

III 1c, 2b, 3a, 4c, 5a, 6b, 7a, 8b, 9a, 10b, 11c, 12b, 13c, 14c, 15c, 16c, 17b, 18b, 19a, 20c

IV 1T, 2T, 3F, 4T, 5F, 6F, 7F, 8T, 9F, 10T, 11F, 12T, 13T, 14T, 15F, 16F, 17F, 18T

V 1b, 2f, 3d, 4a, 5c, 6e, 7g, 8j, 9l, 10i, 11k, 12h, 13n, 14o, 15q, 16r, 17m, 18p, 19s

VI 1b, 2d, 3c, 4a, 5h, 6f, 7e, 8g, 9j, 10l, 11i, 12m, 13k

VII 1 plural, 2 singular, 3 scientist, 4 historian, 5 evolution, 6 prince, 7 princess, 8 empress, 9 abbreviation, 10 headmaster (*Am* principal), 11 studies (education), 12 vocabulary, 13 vowels ... consonants, 14 stress, 15 colon, 16 semi-colon, 17 exclamation mark, 18 inverted commas (quotation marks), 19 dash, 20 apostrophe, 21 parenthesis/-es (brackets), 22 examination (exam, test), 23 homework, 24 spelling, 25 professor (lecturer)

VIII 1 reached (drawn, arrived at, come to), 2 draw, 3 makes (conducts), 4 has, 5 use, 6 spread, 7 pass (fail, take), 8 formed, 9 has, 10 reviewed, 11 underline, 12 do, 13 is, 14 gives (holds) ... attend (go to), 15 give, 16 write (do, have)

IX 1 to, 2 in ... from, 3 on, 4 from, 5 to, 6 in ... of, 7 in, 8 After, 9 in, 10 of, 11 from, 12 Greek ... Roman, 13 in, 14 on, 15 of, 16 for, 17 in, 18 in (at), 19 with (from), 20 at

X 1 essay (composition, paper), 2 justifies, 3 doing, 4 of, 5 exercise (have), 6 pen, 7 comma, 8 pronunciation

How many mistakes have you made?

	I to VI	VII to IX	X	
Excellent	0— 5	0— 6	0	mistakes
Good	6—11	7—12	1	mistakes
Satisfactory	12—18	13—20	2	mistakes
Not very good	19—26	21—31	3—4	mistakes
Weak	over 26	over 31	over 4	mistakes

Chapter XIII The Arts, Films, Radio, Television

You're almost at the end of our book! Have you discovered that you have a *talent for* English?

What will you do in the future? Whatever you do, don't let your knowledge of English *decay!* Try to use it! Do you ever get a chance to *go to* English-language *films?* British and American stage *productions* are world-famous; will you be able to see some? Can your radio get the *BBC* or another English-language *network?* Do your local television stations *televise* English-language films or programmes?

To be fair, we have to warn you: it's terribly easy to forget a foreign language if you don't use it!

I. What's the opposite?

1. Tastes differ; what *displeases* you may
   a) hurt me.
   b) be sour for me.
   c) delight me.

2. I can't *draw from memory.* I have to
   a) be reminded.
   b) enjoy life.
   c) draw from life.

3. Italian art *flourished* in the 15th century and
   a) developed in the 16th.
   b) decayed in the 17th.
   c) flashed brilliantly in the 19th.

4. The shop sells both *brass instruments* and
   a) old instruments.
   b) expensive instruments.
   c) string instruments.

5. Can you *play at sight* or do you
   a) have to work?
   b) have to look it over first?
   c) play only trumpets and horns?

6. Even when she cries, her tears seem to me to be *artificial*, not
   a) shocking.
   b) ugly.
   c) natural.

II. Which word or phrase has almost the same meaning?

1. He has a large *role* in the second act.
   a) circular motion
   b) part
   c) fight scene

2. He made a quick *sketch*.
   a) rough drawing
   b) portrait
   c) small sculpture

3. He was a *gifted* artist.
   a) supported by gifts
   b) generous
   c) talented

4. His latest record seems quite *noteworthy* to me.
   a) worth the notes
   b) worth taking note of
   c) worth paying for

5. She wants to learn *carving*.
   a) digging for buried works of art
   b) designing women's clothes
   c) cutting figures out of wood

6. The *vault* has just been repaired.
   a) church tower
   b) inside of a church
   c) curved roof

7. This report has been *altered*.
   a) changed
   b) made to seem older
   c) used in religious broadcasts

8. The news report had to be *modified*.
   a) changed slightly
   b) brought up-to-date
   c) written in a more exciting way

III. Which choice makes sense?

1. Most children imitate their
   a) parents.
   b) paintings.
   c) parts in a play.

2. The ancient church had a vaulted
   a) organ concert.
   b) history.
   c) roof.

3. We admired the old arched
   a) music.
   b) story.
   c) bridge.

4. "Henry's gone to the cloakroom
   a) to wash his hands."
   b) to get my coat."
   c) to buy something to eat."

5. A bandmaster is the leader of a group of
   a) actors.
   b) singers.
   c) musicians.

6. Jazz began
   a) with Frederic Chopin.
   b) at the Edinburgh Music Festival.
   c) in New Orleans around 1900.

7. It was an unbelievably expensive film to make, with a cast of
   a) three years.
   b) thousands of people.
   c) millions of dollars.

8. In her home the star screened
   a) the script for her next film.
   b) her latest film for friends.
   c) when her husband hit her.

9. The little girl broke the television
   a) screen.
   b) programme.
   c) wave-length.

John Singer Sargent (1856—1925), an American painter who lived most of his life in London and who established a *reputation* as a leading painter of *portraits* and *water-colour landscapes*, once said, "Every time I paint a *portrait* I lose a friend."

IV. Is it true or false?

	T	F
1. Both sculpture and painting are forms of artistic expression.	☐	☐
2. Etching is the fine art of complaining, especially about art.	☐	☐
3. An arch is a straight row of stones, usually forming part of a flat roof.	☐	☐
4. All large portraits are masterpieces.	☐	☐
5. Television networks consist of broadcasting stations which transmit programmes.	☐	☐
6. The wave-length is the amount of time in which a radio speaker must finish his programme.	☐	☐
7. Black-and-white photography was invented before colour photography.	☐	☐
8. A microphone is a very small telephone.	☐	☐

Do you agree?

"*Architecture* is frozen music."
Johann Wolfgang von Goethe (1829)

V. Find the nouns which go together.

1. string instrument
2. brass instrument
3. singer
4. conductor
5. composer
6. receiver

a) Beethoven, b) trumpet, c) loudspeaker, d) violin, e) orchestra, f) voice

7. musician
8. melody
9. chorus
10. gramophone
11. overture
12. wireless
13. box-office

g) opening, h) tune, i) player, j) ticket-sellers, k) radio, l) record-player, m) choir

VI. Find the words which go together.

1. to paint .....
2. to act .....
3. to shoot .....
4. to tune .....
5. to be .....
6. to jam .....

a) a role, b) a landscape, c) musical, d) a broadcast, e) a film, f) an instrument

Do you agree?
"All art is quite useless."
Oscar Wilde (1891)

VII. Put in the right noun.

1. Did you listen to the news on the ..... this morning?
2. The letters 'BBC' stand for .....
3. As soon as we got some extra money we bought a new television .....
4. I heard Leonard Bernstein as guest conductor of the London Symphony .....
5. Violins and trumpets are musical .....
6. A ..... is a person who plays a violin.
7. A person who makes sculptures is a .....
8. "I've seen her act in about ten films, and I think she's a terrible ....."
9. A man who produces films is a .....
10. A man who takes pictures with a camera is a .....
11. Shakespeare's plays were originally performed in an open-air .....
12. We got back to our seats just as the ..... was rising for the third act.
13. Somebody in the audience shouted, "Fire!", and we all ran madly towards the emergency .....

VIII. Put in the right verb.

1. I'm no good with pencils. I can't even ..... a straight line!
2. He hates carrying a camera, but he likes to ..... pictures.
3. The Prime Minister's speech will be ..... on television and radio.
4. His daughter wrote some foolish play which he wants to ..... on the stage.
5. Schubert ..... Goethe's "Erlkönig" to music.
6. I took lessons for about ten years, but I really can't ..... the piano very well.
7. When Beethoven's Third Symphony was first performed in public, the composer ..... the orchestra himself.

IX. Put in the right adjective or preposition.

1. The blue lines stand out nicely ..... the yellow background.
2. Would you rather paint ..... oils or ..... water-colours?
3. He knows a great deal ..... art.
4. I'd say he produced a rather notable work ..... art.
5. Did you see that old film ..... television last night?
6. Come on! Let's go ..... the pictures tonight!
7. Do you think it'll be a black-and-white film or a ..... film?
8. How many copies should I print ..... this negative?
9. He's a good actor; it's a pity he has only a small part ..... the play.
10. She sang while her husband accompanied her ..... the piano.
11. Would you like to hear my daughter play a piece ..... music on the violin?

X. Review: Put in the right word.

1. I'm afraid your daughter ..... not at all musical.
2. Do you know who wrote the ..... of that film?
3. "No, I've never seen this music before, but I can play almost anything ..... sight."
4. Can you draw ..... memory?
5. I don't think the station broadcasts on this wave-.....
6. A person who writes symphonies is a .....
7. We bought the theatre tickets yesterday at the .....-office.
8. Did you listen ..... the news this morning?

It's time again to check your answers!

Key

I 1c, 2c, 3b, 4c, 5b, 6c

II 1b, 2a, 3c, 4b, 5c, 6c, 7a, 8a

III 1a, 2c, 3c, 4b, 5c, 6c, 7b, 8b, 9a

IV 1T, 2F, 3F, 4F, 5T, 6F, 7T, 8F

V 1d, 2b, 3f, 4e, 5a, 6c, 7i, 8h, 9m, 10l, 11g, 12k, 13j

VI 1b, 2a, 3e, 4f, 5c, 6d

VII 1 wireless (radio), 2 British Broadcasting Corporation, 3 set, 4 Orchestra, 5 instruments, 6 violinist, 7 sculptor, 8 actress, 9 producer, 10 photographer (*false:* photograph; *with a film camera:* cameraman), 11 theatre, 12 curtain, 13 exit

VIII 1 draw, 2 take, 3 broadcast, 4 put, 5 set, 6 play, 7 conducted

IX 1 against, 2 in (with) ... in (with), 3 about, 4 of, 5 on, 6 to, 7 colour, 8 from, 9 in, 10 on, 11 of

X 1 is, 2 script, 3 at, 4 from, 5 length, 6 composer, 7 box, 8 to

How many mistakes have you made?

	I to VI	VII to IX	X
Excellent	0— 3	0— 3	0 mistakes
Good	4— 6	4— 6	1 mistakes
Satisfactory	7— 9	7—10	2 mistakes
Not very good	10—13	11—16	3—4 mistakes
Weak	over 13	over 16	over 4 mistakes

We hope you haven't been *displeased* by our efforts to help you develop a feeling for English. But this is the end; now we can only wish you good luck!